SPIRITS, GODS AND MAGIC

AN INTRODUCTION TO THE ANTHROPOLOGY OF THE SUPERNATURAL

SPIRITS, GODS AND MAGIC

AN INTRODUCTION TO THE ANTHROPOLOGY OF THE SUPERNATURAL

by

Jack Hunter

Foreword by Fiona Bowie

Afterword by David Luke

www.augustnightpress.com

CONTENTS

⌣

A BRIEF NOTE ON THIS EDITION

JACK HUNTER

~

This book was written in the winter of 2011-12 at a relatively early stage in my academic career, eight years ago by the time this new edition is published. It was initially intended to be an introduction to the anthropology of religion and the supernatural aimed at those with an interest in parapsychology and the paranormal, but I hope it will also be of interest to a broader readership. I felt such a book was needed because the anthropological literature contains a wealth of information about the social and cultural context of paranormal experiences that is often neglected in the paranormal research community. Laboratory-based parapsychology, for example, has often approached paranormal phenomena from what could be considered a 'reductionist' perspective - attempting to break paranormal experiences down into their most basic components in order to understand them. Such an approach is necessary, of course, to objectively demonstrate the existence of psi phenomena - extra-sensory perception (ESP), telepathy, psychokinesis (PK) - to isolate the phenomena in the lab and rule out the possibility of sensory information leakage from mundane sources. It has been a relatively successful approach, yielding statistical evidence for the existence of subtle psi effects (see the discussion in Chapter Six), but it leaves out a large part of the way in which such experiences and phenomena manifest and are experienced in the real world - in the midst of the dramas of social life and filtered through cultural norms and expectations. As we will see throughout the pages of this book, manifestations of psi and the paranormal in real-life contexts are often far more powerful, bizarre and complex than anything recorded in parapsychological laboratories (see in particular Chapter Five). This book, then, seeks to re-dress the balance by considering paranormal phenomena through the broader - more holistic - frameworks of social anthropology and related disciplines.

In the time since this book was originally published my work and ideas have developed along trajectories that I could not have imagined when I originally sat down to write it. For example, my most recent edited collection, *Greening the Paranormal*,[1] is an exploration of extraordinary experience and ecology. By taking the ecological context of extraordinary experiences into account *Greening the Paranormal* expands the social and cultural dimensions of the paranormal (such as are discussed in this book), to include our embeddedness in wider networks of interaction with the natural world, which surrounds and sustains us. These ideas are not covered in this book, though it is clear to see how they emerged from the perspectives that are explored in these pages. On a related note, my forthcoming monograph *Manifesting Spirits*[2] presents my doctoral research with a contemporary trance mediumship development circle in Bristol in its entirety. Many of the ideas it builds on are briefly explored in this book (in particular in the sections on spirit possession in Chapter Three), but are much more thoroughly examined in *Manifesting Spirits*. Similarly, the ideas explored in Chapter Seven of this book have been elaborated in several different places over the intervening years. Perhaps the chief development has been my concept of 'ontological flooding' - an approach that emphasises the complexity of the paranormal (or any other phenomenon) and suggests the need to entertain multiple simultaneous explanatory frameworks if we hope to understand it - which is only vaguely hinted at in this book. A more complete explanation of the idea is presented in the introduction to the edited volume *Damned Facts*,[3] the book *Engaging the Anomalous*,[4] and in other chapters and articles I have written since this book was first published. Suffice to say that if you are interested in pursuing any of these lines of inquiry further please check out some of these other publications, as well as the references included at the end of this book.

There have also been recent developments in anthropology that are worth briefly mentioning here, as they are not fully discussed in the chapters that follow. One such development is the so-called 'ontological turn' in anthropology, which suggests that we are not simply dealing with 'cultures' and 'beliefs' when we engage with and participate in the lives of our fieldwork informants. Instead, we are dealing with entirely different *worlds*, that might be completely alien to our own. The realisation that there are many worlds beyond that presented by Western materialist science calls for a radical readjustment of anthropological research and the methods and theories employed to make sense of it. Martin Holbraad and Morten Pedersen, two pioneers of the ontological turn, have gone so far as to suggest that anthropological concepts will have to be "modulated or transformed" in order to effectively articulate these other worlds.[5] Others have suggested that this process might involve the adoption of local and indigenous concepts into anthropological theory, a rejection of representationalist perspectives, and an emphasis on the extended mind hypothesis.[6] Some of the ideas discussed in this book might also be part of this ontological turn in anthropology.

As the title suggests, then, this book should be treated as an introduction to the anthropology of the supernatural - as a pointer for further reading and exploration. Think about it as a sort of foundation course - a starting place. It is intended to be a relatively easy read and to be encouraging of researchers, old and new, to expand their perspectives and take the study of the paranormal in new directions. I sincerely hope that you find it interesting!

Jack Hunter
January 2020

FOREWORD

FIONA BOWIE

~

'In all chaos there is a cosmos, in all disorder a secret order.'

—CARL G. JUNG (1897-1961)

In the above quotation Swiss psychologist, psychoanalyst and mystic, Carl Jung, is referring to the archetype of the *anima*, the life force that belongs to the realm of the gods and metaphysics; the force that breaks down the carefully constructed walls of convention and control in its thirst for life and urge just to be. Chaos, according to Jung, invokes a sense of terror and dissolution, reminiscent of the symbolic death of the shaman undergoing initiation, a death that is no less real for being invisible to the outer eyes. The realization that life itself might be meaningless, that there is no purpose to existence other than existence itself, is perhaps the most terrifying descent into hell that any human being can experience. But the *anima* is also linked to the archetype of order, and to an ancient form of thought in which consciousness does not so much think as *perceive*. The inner world is sensed as external phenomena and experienced as revelation, 'not invented but forced upon us or brining conviction through its immediacy and actuality

An anthropology of the supernatural is centrally concerned with this search for meaning in the midst of chaos. It charts the efforts of human beings to interpret the signs, symbols and archetypes that arise in dreams, which present themselves in visions, and which are described by the shaman, medium or mystic.

In clear, concise language Jack Hunter introduces the reader to some of the key theories, personalities and concepts in the anthropology of religion, particularly as they relate to notions of the supernatural. As Hunter points out, the term 'supernatural' is rather problematic, being based on Western presuppositions that there is a distinction between a natural and a supernatural order (often explicitly or implicitly regarded respectively as real and unreal), that is not shared by most peoples in most historical periods. Familiar topics such as witchcraft, shamanism and spirit possession are succinctly presented with the aid of historical and cross-cultural examples. The chief innovation of this Introduction, however, is the inclusion of a chapter on 'Ethnography and the Paranormal,' a subject Hunter is particularly well qualified to write about as founder and editor of the groundbreaking journal *Paranthropology*, and a co-founder of the Afterlife Research Centre. Although interest in the paranormal goes back to the early years of anthropological endeavor, it has only recently re-emerged as a valid object of ethnographic inquiry and a promising sub-discipline within the anthropology of religion, and related disciplines.

The paranormal is also the area that brings into sharpest focus the relationship between internal and external worlds, the realm of imagination and the forces of nature. Indeed, it confounds attempts to draw firm boundaries between these two aspects of human experience. Like the *anima*, discussions of the paranormal both destroy and reconfigure meaning. Anomalous experiences that challenge rigid boundaries may be unsettling, but they also contain the seeds of an integrated view of the self and enlarged vision of the cosmos. Anthropology is generally more concerned with questions of interpretation than whether phenomena are objectively real, but by attempting to forge links between ethnographic and parapsychological approaches to the supernatural, areas that used to be much closer to one another than they are today, Hunter inevitably brings ontological as well as hermeneutical questions to the fore. This brief volume is therefore to be welcomed both for its adept discussion of familiar topics and its equally sure handling of areas at the cutting edge of contemporary anthropological and interdisciplinary inquiry.

INTRODUCTION

~

Human societies exist side-by-side with an invisible world. For as long as we have been able to express ourselves, through spoken words, images and writing, we have documented and described encounters with phenomena that seem to transcend the everyday world of mundane things, and hint at the existence of a universe populated by innumerable minds, powerful forces and mysterious phenomena. This is the world that has come to be called 'supernatural,' a term which, etymologically, suggests something above, or transcending, the natural order of reality. As a discipline concerned with understanding human beings, anthropology has, since its inception in the nineteenth century, been expressly concerned with trying to understand, interpret and explain human beliefs in the existence of spirits, gods and magical powers. Such beliefs have been a challenge to anthropologists because they seem to fly in the face of both everyday experience and the canons of Western rationalist science, which has actively constructed itself in opposition to notions of the supernatural. Nevertheless, such experiences and beliefs remain extremely persistent, widespread and fundamental to many of the world's cultures. This book is an introduction to anthropological approaches to the study of the supernatural.

What is anthropology?

The simplest definition comes from dissecting the word 'anthropology' itself, which is composed of two separate Greek words: *anthrōpos*, meaning 'human' or 'human being,' and -logia, meaning 'study.'

Anthropology is, in essence, therefore, the study of humankind. But what exactly does the study of human beings entail? In the American tradition, anthropology has generally been split into four separate sub-disciplines each focusing on different aspects of human existence, and these can give us a good idea of the sorts of things that anthropologists are interested in. The four sub-disciplines include: physical (or biological) anthropology, being concerned with the evolutionary development of human beings; archaeology, dealing with the material culture and remains of past human societies; linguistic anthropology, which is concerned with the development and use of languages by human beings; and cultural anthropology, which examines the varieties of human cultures and their influence on society and the individual. In the British tradition cultural anthropology is often referred to as social anthropology and shares many ancestral commonalities with European sociology, and usually takes the methodological approach known as ethnography as its starting point. This book will be primarily concerned with social and cultural anthropology, though it will also branch out into the other sub-fields as and when the need arises.

What is the Supernatural?

The *Oxford English Dictionary* defines the term 'supernatural' as referring to 'a manifestation or event attributed to some force beyond scientific understanding or the laws of nature.' But what sort of things do we label as supernatural? The word *supernaturalis* was first used by medieval theologians in the thirteenth century to refer to the extraordinary events described in the Bible - from Moses' parting of the Red Sea, to Jesus Christ's curing of the sick, aquatic perambulations and eventual resurrection. So in its earliest usage the term was intimately connected with the idea of miracles, which are unusual events believed to have been caused by God with the aim of producing faith in witnesses.[7] A lot has changed since the thirteenth century, however, and now the term supernatural is used to refer to a much wider range of events and ideas: from allegedly haunted houses and ghosts to flying saucers and visitors from other worlds. The term has also been used by anthropologists, since the nineteenth century, to refer to the beliefs and practices of human beings throughout the world as they relate to notions of spirits, magic, witchcraft and religion. In the context of this book the word 'supernatural' will be used in its broadest sense to refer to all of the examples just mentioned, encompassing many varied ideas concerning gods, spirits and magic.

Extraordinary or Ordinary?

It is important to remember, however, that the concept of the supernatural is both a distinctly modern and specifically European one, established on the premise that there are immutable laws that govern the natural world, and that such things as magic, miracles and spirits must, in some way, be separate and distinct from those laws, hence 'super-natural.'[8] As a consequence they are considered 'extraordinary,' 'abnormal,' 'un-natural,' and so on. A good example of this assumption in action can be seen in the contemporary Western debate about the 'paranormal,' which is defined as referring to events that are considered to be 'beyond the scope of current scientific understanding.' According to the dominant Western scientific paradigm - essentially a form of materialist reductionism - paranormal events are simply not possible because they breach fundamentally accepted laws of nature (as defined by science). A useful illustration of this approach to defining away certain phenomena and experiences is found in the Enlightenment philosopher David Hume's (1711-1776) definition of a miracle as a 'transgression of a law of nature by the volition of the Deity, or by the intervention of some invisible agent.'[9] As Hume's understanding of the laws of nature is of eternal, fixed and unchanging physical laws, any transgression of such laws is impossible by definition. In this way Hume essentially defines miracles away.

In thinking about the supernatural beliefs of other peoples around the world, however, we need to be wary of the fact that within different cultural settings the category of the supernatural, as we understand it, does not necessarily exist. Spirits, gods, magic and witchcraft may be thought of as just as much a part of the natural world as the trees, rocks, rivers and mountains, and although experiences of such things as ghosts and spirits may be relatively rare, and are distinguished from the mundane experience of daily life, they are certainly not thought to be impossible, or to be somehow beyond classification as natural, normal or ordinary. Indeed they may constitute a very important element of a particular culture's worldview.

Why Take an Anthropological Approach?

All too often paranormal experiences and supernatural beliefs in modern Euro-American culture are thought about in isolation from other related experiences and beliefs in different societies. For example, in popular media portrayals of, say, spirit mediumship, we are only likely to be exposed to the types of mediumship practiced in the European and American Spiritualist movement. We might see, for example, depictions of fraudulent mediums levitating tables in darkened Victorian séance rooms, or well-groomed spirit mediums giving statements about the deceased relatives of audience members on stage in a brightly lit television studio. Such stereotypes are, of course, quite specific to European culture and should not be taken as representative of spirit mediumship in the cross-cultural context. Indeed, sticking with this example for a little longer, spirit mediumship (as we shall see in a later chapter), comes in a huge variety of forms in different cultures across the globe.[10] The same applies to beliefs about ghosts and spirits, or magic and witchcraft - what we take for granted about them is not necessary taken for granted in other cultures. This book, then, aims to situate such experiences and beliefs within a much broader framework through taking a cross-cultural and comparative approach. It is hoped that this approach will not only give the reader a greater appreciation of the variety of supernatural beliefs and paranormal experiences prevalent in the world's cultures, but also that it will allow for a more in-depth, and so better informed, appreciation of similar issues within Euro-American culture. By taking a cross-cultural approach and comparing different traditions we can move towards a greater understanding of what is really going on in these experiences. We can develop new theories and models to help us make sense of them, while also discovering what such experiences mean to those who have them, and how they are incorporated into different ways of looking at the world.

Types of Evidence

We will encounter many different types of evidence throughout this book, from ethnographic descriptions of traditional beliefs, through anecdotal accounts of personal experiences, to experimental data gathered in controlled laboratory settings. All of these different forms of evidence have different degrees of acceptance in Western science, with experimental laboratory data given the most credibility and anecdotal reports the least credibility. Philosopher and parapsychologist Stephen Braude has suggested three categories of evidence for the so-called paranormal: *experimental, semi-experimental* and *anecdotal.* According to this categorization, semi-experimental evidence would refer to data, 'including accounts of lived experience' that consist of 'claims that cannot be readily obtained at will, but are sufficiently numerous to be worthy of being included in serious theorizing.' The idea is, therefore, that although unlike laboratory based experimental evidence that can supposedly be replicated at will; claims to experiences outside the controlled conditions of the lab can still be treated as valid data so long as they are sufficiently recursive.[11] The sheer quantity of ethnographic accounts and first-hand experiential narratives could, therefore, be classed under Braude's category of 'semi-experimental evidence,' and in this respect, at the very least, seem to indicate that there is *something* going on when it comes to the paranormal. With this in mind, let's take our first tentative steps into the paranormal multiverse and see what we might find.

CHAPTER 1

TRENDS IN THE ANTHROPOLOGY OF THE SUPERNATURAL

~

The branch of anthropology that is most concerned with the supernatural is the anthropology of religion, a sub-field of social and cultural anthropology. Religion has been a key concern for anthropologists since the very dawn of the discipline in the mid-nineteenth century. In light of the apparent diversity of forms that religion takes throughout the world, from the monotheism characteristic of Christianity, Judaism and Islam, to the polytheism of Hinduism and Buddhism, and all the many varieties in between, one of the first tasks facing the early anthropologists was to develop a standard definition of religion. At first glance this might seem like an easy task, but a generally accepted definition has, even today, yet to be devised. The problem lies in the complexity of the various phenomena usually categorised as religious in nature, and in understanding how all of these disparate parts relate to one another. For example, religion may be defined in terms of the beliefs of a certain people, or in terms of their practices, that is their rituals, rites and performances. Religion might also be interpreted politically and economically, or described using the language of psychology and philosophy. This complexity, combined with huge cultural variation, makes the development of an all-encompassing definition and theory of religion a particularly difficult task, which has consequently led to a plethora of scholarly perspectives.[12] Over the course of this chapter we will examine several of the major definitions and theories proposed by anthropologists, sociologists and other scholars of religion, with the aim that they might help us when grappling with the main subject matter of this book, the so-called paranormal.

Defining Religion

Edward Burnett Tylor (1832-1917), widely regarded as one of the founding fathers of modern anthropology, realised that any definition of religion would have to be inclusive of the broad spectrum of religious ideas present throughout the human world. Tylor was shocked to read, in the reports of pioneering explorers and missionaries, that many newly 'discovered' societies were described as possessing no religion at all, despite their apparent preoccupation with spirits, demons and ancestors. This neglect, he thought, arose from too narrow a definition of what religion entails, arguing that if our definition of religion is based on the notion of belief in a supreme deity, judgement after death, or the adoration of idols (which are hallmarks of both classical and contemporary European religions), the beliefs of a great many non-European people would immediately be excluded from the category of religion. To Tylor this simply did not make sense. The problem with this sort of definition was that it was based upon a *particular development* of religion - namely a Judeo-Christian development - and not upon religion itself. In order to counter this, Tylor defined religion, in its simplest terms, as 'the belief in spiritual beings' – a common trait across religions that he found ample evidence of in the ethnographic documents he read. Tylor's definition of religion, therefore, highlighted the significance of *belief*, as well as the supernatural objects of these beliefs - spirits, ancestors, demons and deities.[13]

Another influential definition of religion was offered by Émile Durkheim (1858-1917), a pioneering sociologist and contemporary of Tylor's, who argued that belief in spiritual beings, although common to many religions, could not be considered a *minimum definition* of religion because there are religious systems that do not hold such beings as centrally important to their faith. To illustrate this point Durkheim gives the example of Buddhism, which does not consider gods and spirits to be central to its beliefs (though it does not exclude them), but rather emphasises the Buddha's Four Noble Truths as its main creed (*dukkha* - 'suffering,' *samudaya* - 'craving,' *nirodha* - 'the end of suffering,' and the Eightfold Path to end suffering). It is for this reason that Buddhism is sometimes thought of as a philosophy, rather than as a religion. Durkheim suggested, therefore, that religion could best be defined as a unified system of beliefs and practices relative to 'sacred things' and as beliefs and practices that unite its adherents in a 'single moral community.' To Durkheim, then, religion was to do with the sacred, which he defined as things set apart and surrounded by prohibitions and taboos. For Durkheim, then, the sacred did not have to include supernatural concepts or references to spirits or gods. Durkheim's definition of religion could, for example, equally be applied to other social phenomena, as long as they were treated with a special kind of respect and separated from normal everyday life by certain prohibitions. Above all, Durkheim thought of religion as a social and communal phenomenon - that the sacred is created by humans through collective ritual. From this perspective religion is more about what people do than what they believe.[14] We will hear more about the influence of Durkheim's functionalist view of religion shortly.

A more recent definition of religion was been proposed by the anthropologist Clifford Geertz (1926-2006), who suggests that religion is primarily a symbolic cultural system. For Geertz religion is a set of symbols that perform particular functions within a society. Geertz's definition reads:

> Religion is (1) a system of symbols, which (2) acts to establish powerful, pervasive and long-lasting moods and motivations in men by (3) formulating conceptions of a general order of existence and (4) clothing these conceptions with such an aura of factuality that (5) the moods and motivations seem uniquely realistic.[15]

In considering religion as a set of symbols, Geertz shifts the focus of defining religion away from purely sociological and psychological factors (though these are also included in his definition) towards a more holistic view of the phenomenon. Geertz emphasises religion as a *lived in system*, comprising the world-view of its adherents, shaping their experience and interpretation of the world.

A complete survey of all the various scholarly attempts at defining religion exceeds the scope of this book, but suffice to say that any comprehensive definition of religion will have to be *inclusive* of a broad range of supernatural conceptualisations, address social, psychological and symbolic factors, while also emphasising the holistic, and embedded, nature of any given religious world-view in the lives of its adherents.

Religion is much more than dogma, liturgy and scripture. Indeed, the scholar of religion Ninian Smart (1927-2001) identified seven key 'dimensions' of religion:

1. The Practical and Ritual Dimension (Ritual and Practice)
2. The Experiential and Emotional Dimension (Experiences and Emotions)
3. The Narrative Dimension (Stories)
4. The Doctrinal and Philosophical Dimension (Philosophy and Theology)
5. The Ethical and Legal Dimension (Laws)
6. The Social and Institutional Dimension (Social Functions)
7. The Material Dimension (Art and Architecture).[16]

This is one of the most useful frameworks for encapsulating the complexity of religion, demonstrating how the various strands and functions of religion coalesce to create something that is much more than the sum of its constituent parts, and cannot be reduced to any single one of them.

Theories for the Origins of Religion

Perhaps more pertinent to the subject of this book - the anthropology of the supernatural - than definitions of religion are the various theories that have been proposed for the origin of religion, because these theories seek to explain how and why religion arises in the first place. In his book *Theories of Primitive Religion*, anthropologist E.E. Evans-Pritchard (1902-1973), divided such theories into two distinct sets: psychological theories and sociological theories, and these categories are still broadly applicable today.[17] For the benefit of simplicity, then, we will look at a selection of anthropological theories for the origin of religion from within Evans-Pritchard's framework, and will begin with the psychological theories.

1) Psychological and Cognitive Theories

As we have already seen, E.B. Tylor's minimum definition of religion was the belief in spiritual beings. He called this belief *animism* - from the Latin root word *anima* meaning 'soul' - and suggested that it was from this 'primitive' belief in the existence of spirits that all religious ideas ultimately stemmed. Tylor suggested that the idea of supernatural beings could effectively be explained away as the misinterpretation of experiences such as dreaming and trance states. For example, Tylor argued that early humans might have mistaken their encounters with deceased acquaintances in dreams as real meetings with real people. From such experiences early humans posited the existence of a non-physical component of the person that could continue to exist after the death of the physical body, and so reach out to them in dreams. Tylor further reasoned that primitive humans expanded this idea out to other aspects of the world: attributing spirits, or souls, to animals, plants and other natural phenomena such as the wind, lightning, mountains, rivers and the sun (amongst many other natural phenomena), which often seem to possess a consciousness of their own. Tylor's animism, therefore, suggests that supernatural beliefs arise from an attempt to make sense of unusual experiences and to explain the seemingly conscious activities of animals, plants and other natural phenomena. It is for this reason that Tylor's theory is often described as an 'intellectualist' theory - religion arises out of a misguided (unscientific and irrational) attempt to make sense of the world around us.

Another quite different psychological theory of religion is the psychological functionalism of Bronislaw Malinowski (1884-1942). For Malinowski, supernatural beliefs developed out of a need for psychological stability in an unpredictable world. To illustrate this point Malinowski considered the performance of fertility rituals amongst the Trobriand Islanders of Papua New Guinea, with whom he conducted fieldwork. Malinowski suggests that these rituals serve the important function of reassuring the individual that they have done all that is within their power to ensure a good harvest, especially once all practical and technological methods have been applied. Malinowski is eager to point out, however, that dependence upon magic is not evidence of a lack of 'scientific' knowledge, but rather insists that magical rituals are *complementary* to empirical knowledge.[18] Supernatural beliefs, according to this functionalist perspective, serve an evolutionary purpose in enabling humans to better cope with the psychological stresses of everyday life. They are, therefore, purely psychological phenomena, and might best be understood as psychological defense mechanisms.

Taking a similarly psychological stance, structuralist anthropology, as pioneered by the French anthropologist Claude Levi-Strauss

(1908-2009), seeks to understand human culture in terms of deep structures within the human mind. These structures inform the way in which we experience the world around us, and become apparent in our cultural constructs.[19] The classic example of such a 'deep structure' is the propensity towards interpreting the world through binary oppositions: positive and negative; good and evil; light and dark; hot and cold; raw and cooked; clean and unclean, and so on. For Levi-Strauss, then, religions, and mythology more specifically, are cultural manifestations of the underlying structures of the human mind. By dissecting the religious and mythical systems that human minds have developed we can, in turn, gain access to these deep structures of consciousness. From this perspective, religious and mythological systems represent a means of understanding the world through symbols and conceptual constructs that have their roots deep within human consciousness, and are expressions, at a very fundamental level, of the way in which we categorise, make sense of, and understand the world around us.

Similarly, cognitive theories seek to understand religion as the result of innate functions within the human mind. In certain respects cognitive approaches can be seen as descendants of Tylor's approach, which considers supernatural concepts to be the product of misunderstood but otherwise natural experiences such as sleep and trance, but they also bear important similarities to structuralist theories. One of the most influential cognitive theorists of religion is the anthropologist Stewart Guthrie, who has put forward the hypothesis that the innate human propensity for recognising patterns in random formations (for example seeing faces in the clouds), ultimately led to the belief that the world was populated by other minds similar to our own.[20] This is often referred to as the hyperactive agency detection hypothesis.[21] The theory essentially suggests that the ability to recognise agents (minds with intentionality) in the environment has been selected for by evolutionary processes because it allows us to spot potential predators in the wild, thus improving chances for survival. The belief in supernatural beings arose when this useful skill for detecting potentially dangerous predators was mistakenly applied to other natural phenomena that do not possess consciousness, for example drawing the conclusion that lightning must be conscious because it moves. Like Tylor's theory, then, Guthrie's cognitive theory emphasises the misattribution of consciousness to non-conscious natural phenomena, and like Levi-Strauss' structuralism cognitive theories understand religion as an expression of innate processes deep within the human mind.

2) Sociological Theories

Sociological theories of religion are not concerned with the experiences of individuals as such, rather their emphasis is on the social group and the role that religion might perform within it. Compared to the psychological theories discussed above, which could be conceived a 'bottom up' theories (moving from the individual to society), sociological theories often present 'top down' perspectives (from society to the individual). Sociological theories of religion can also be broadly categorised as functionalist in that they tend to focus on understanding what it is that religion *does* for individuals and social groups.

Émile Durkheim's writings are usually regarded as foundational texts in the development of sociological theories of religion. As we have already seen, Durkheim conceived of religion as a purely *social* phenomenon, and was not primarily concerned with trying to understand the nature of the experiences that gave rise to it (though even these he suggests are experiences of the social). For Durkheim religion, in its very essence, was a sort of social mechanism aimed at maintaining group cohesion. In other words, through providing a group of people with a distinct set of beliefs, religion enables distinctive cultures to develop with their own shared norms, values, symbols and sense of social identity. This shared identity would include, for example, belief in the same gods and performance of the same rituals, and would ultimately lead to a stronger, more unified, society.

The British anthropologist A.R. Radcliffe-Brown (1881-1955) drew on Durkheim's sociological interpretation to develop what he termed the structural-functionalist approach to understanding social systems. According to Radcliffe-Brown's model, human societies can be thought of as consisting of many interrelated component parts (or social systems), which combine to produce a fully functioning whole, much like a living organism.[22] Social institutions, such as religion, are therefore interpreted as components in the social organism that serve to ensure that it does not fall apart. For Radcliffe-Brown it was not the beliefs of a society that were important, rather it was their rites and rituals - what people do - because it is the performance of rituals that brings the social group together. Indeed, he suggested, contrary to the approaches of psychological theorists (who tended towards the position that rituals developed from specific supernatural beliefs), that it was the performance of essential rituals (such as the burial of the dead), that were ultimately explained and given meaning by the development of supernatural beliefs. According to Radcliffe-Brown, the origins of religion can be seen in the necessary rituals performed by human groups: ritual comes first, followed by explanatory beliefs. From this perspective, then, religion is nothing more than a specialised social process with no underlying reality other than its sociological and structural efficacy.

3) Phenomenological and Other Theories

Unlike the psychological and sociological theories outlined above, which essentially suggest that there is no underlying reality to religious and paranormal experiences (other than their psychological and sociological functions), phenomenological approaches do not jump quite so quickly to such conclusions. Indeed, phenomenological approaches often ignore, or bracket out, the question of the reality of the experience under investigation in order to focus on the experience itself. In other words, phenomenological approaches treat experience *as* experience, without attempting to explain it away. Such approaches place a significant emphasis on understanding what is often called *religious experience*, considering it an irreducible category in itself, and an essential component in understanding religious belief and practice.

Prior to the nineteenth century the term 'religious experience' was used primarily in a theological context. Religious experience was something that happened within the framework of established religion, and as such was not investigated by social scientists like psychologists or sociologists. The American psychologist and philosopher William James (1842-1910) was one of the first to discuss religious experience from a perspective external to theology. James considered religious experience to be a distinct class of experience that he pragmatically defined by its fruits, or the moral transformation it produces in the experiencer. He reasoned that the characteristics of 'philosophical reasonableness and moral helpfulness,' when resulting directly from a religious experience, should be taken as evidence in favour of defining that experience as genuinely religious in nature.

As a psychologist James was most interested in the private thoughts and feelings associated with religious experience. He did not consider religious experiences to be 'supernatural,' but rather a natural fact of human life. In James' view religious belief systems developed around individuals who had encountered religious experiences directly. James took a phenomenological approach to his investigations; compiling numerous narrative accounts of religious experiences in his classic book *The Varieties of Religious Experience*.[23] As part of his phenomenological approach, James undertook a comparative analysis of experiential narratives collected from those he considered 'most accomplished in the religious life,' and highlighted the similarities between their accounts of religious, spiritual and mystical experiences. He identified four key characteristics of religious experiences, suggesting that they are:

1. *Ineffable* - they cannot adequately be put into words.
2. *Noetic* - they impart knowledge, often of God or the ultimate reality.
3. *Transient* - they are short-lived and temporary.
4. *Passive* - they feel like they are coming from outside of the experiencer.

In noting these similarities James was proposing what has come to be called the 'common core hypothesis': the idea that there is a fairly standard kind of 'religious experience' that is interpreted differently according to the experiencer's cultural background. This is an idea we will return to shortly.

Rudolph Otto (1869-1937) was a German theologian and philosopher with a particular interest in the issue of religious experience. Having travelled extensively, Otto was aware of the role of religious experience in non-Christian traditions and so had a wider perspective than many of his contemporaries in theology. Otto's most influential contribution to the study of religious experience was his book *The Idea of the Holy*, first published in 1917. In the book Otto attempts to explore what he calls the non-rational element of the 'holy,' that is the element of the notion that is free from morality, goodness and other modern additions to the idea. Beneath this cultural baggage, Otto suggests, lies a 'unique original feeling response, which can be in itself ethically neutral.' Otto uses the term 'numen,' or 'numinous,' to describe this sensation. For Otto, the numinous possessed a dual nature, at once beautiful and terrifying. He referred to these two aspects as the *mysterium fascinans* (beautiful mystery) and the *mysterium tremendum* (terrifying mystery), and saw these as fundamental components of the religious experience. In distinguishing between the numinous experience and subsequent rational conceptualisations of it, Otto suggests that at its most fundamental level, religion is concerned with a particular kind of experience, and as such cannot truly be understood without an appreciation of it.

The same might also be said of other forms of supernatural belief. David J. Hufford's examination of the Newfoundland 'Old Hag' tradition (in which a person asleep in bed is assaulted by a supernatural being, often in the form of an old witch), is a classic example of a phenomenological approach to the study of supernatural beliefs and experiences.[25] Hufford argued in favour of the 'experiential source hypothesis' as a useful tool in the study of supernatural belief traditions, suggesting that rather than being purely the product of cultural influence, supernatural beliefs often have some basis in lived human experience, regardless of whether that experience was genuinely supernatural or not. For example, the Old Hag may be explained with recourse to sleep paralysis. The Scottish folklorist and anthropologist Andrew Lang (1844-1912) argued along similar lines. Lang suggested, in contrast to Tylor's misinterpretation theory, that supernatural beliefs might have their foundations in genuine anomalous experiences. Indeed, in his book *The Making of Religion*, Lang went so far as to hypothesize that paranormal experiences might have been major contributing factors in the early development of religious ideas. In other words, Lang suggested that supernatural beliefs need not be considered irrational if they were founded upon genuine paranormal experiences, rather than on misinterpreted experiences. Lang opts, therefore, for an approach that takes seriously the possibility of ontologically real supernatural phenomena and beings.[26]

More recently, the anthropologist Edith Turner (1921-2016) has called for an approach to the study of ritual that takes seriously the beliefs and experiences of informants when conducting ethnographic fieldwork. Following her own unusual experiences during a healing ceremony in Zambia (see Chapter Five for a detailed account), Turner concluded that in order to truly understand and appreciate a particular belief system the anthropologist must learn to 'see what the native sees' through a process of active and emotional participation in their belief system and rituals.[27]

The approaches employed by the likes of Otto, James, Lang, Hufford and Turner lead to an appreciation of the significant role of direct personal experience in the development of religious and supernatural belief systems. Unlike the psychological and sociological approaches discussed above, phenomenological theorists do not attempt to 'explain them away' in overly reductionist terms. The shift towards a serious appreciation of subjective experiences in anthropology was a gradual one, inspired in many cases by the personal experiences of anthropologists themselves in the field. Some notable examples will be discussed in greater detail in Chapter Five, and we will return to the development of anthropological approaches to the paranormal in Chapter Seven.

Summary

It is clear from the brief overview of theories and models presented in this chapter that the task of interpreting and understanding humanity's supernatural beliefs is a particularly difficult one. There is a constant tension between those theorists who take a psychological approach, focusing on the experiences and thoughts of the individual, and those who take a sociological approach, with an emphasis on the function that supernatural concepts and their associated practices perform for the wider community. It seems clear, however, that each approach has something significant to offer to our understanding, but that neither taken alone is able to provide a complete explanation. The complexity of the issue at hand demands that we take a more pluralistic approach that emphasises the interaction between social and psychological functions, but that is also open to an examination of the phenomenology of the supernatural (that is how the supernatural is experienced), and the implications of such experiences. We will return to the theories discussed in this opening chapter throughout the book, as they relate to the themes of each individual chapter, and will conclude with an examination of the implications of taking the phenomenology of the supernatural seriously in the two closing chapters.

CHAPTER 2

GHOSTS, SPIRITS, GODS AND DEMONS

~

As we have already seen, it was the global distribution of beliefs in the existence of supernatural beings that prompted the first great anthropological theory for the origin of religion. Tylor called this theory 'animism' and suggested that the belief in spiritual beings was the earliest, most fundamental, form of religion: all systems of religion, so Tylor thought, feature belief in some form of spiritual being. This chapter introduces the topic of humanity's widespread belief in supernatural beings, and the spirit-worlds they inhabit, through an exploration of different cultural ideas about ghosts, spirits, gods and demons, and presents some of the theories that have been proposed to explain such beliefs by anthropologists and ethnographers working in the field.

What are Ghosts, Spirits and Souls?

Popular Western ideas about ghosts are likely to feature mysterious shadowy figures glimpsed in haunted houses, or the shrouded spectres of dead nuns roaming long disused corridors in ancient Abbeys. These are images that are familiar to us because they are deeply rooted in our popular culture, in our ghost stories and horror movies.[28] The idea of the ghost, in Euro-American society, is usually associated with deceased people, indeed a standard dictionary definition of ghost might read something like: 'an apparition of a dead person which is believed to appear or become manifest to the living.' The word 'ghost' itself derives from the Old English term *gāst*, and is related to the German word *geist* meaning spirit or mind. When we use the word ghost, then, we are referring to the spirit or mind of a person that has become separated from the physical body, usually by death.

The term 'spirit' has its origins in the Latin word *spiritus*, meaning breath (as in respiration), and so may be thought of as the life-force of a living being. When a living being dies it ceases to breathe, it no longer possesses breath, its *spiritus* has left the body. In the modern English usage the term spirit refers to the non-physical part of a person and the centre of consciousness and personality of a human - or other - being. Not all spirits move on to the spirit-world. Some remain attached to the physical, often because they have some sort of unfinished business amongst the living, and these spirits become 'ghosts.' A good example of such ghosts can be found in the traditional Japanese Buddhist belief in *Gaki*, described as the spirits of jealous and greedy people who must suffer the punishment of eternal hunger. Similar ghosts are present throughout the Buddhist world and are known as *Preta* in India and *Egui* China.

Another term that commonly gets mixed in amongst these already confusing words is soul. Again, this is a word with Germanic roots, related to the Old English term *sāwol*, and the German word *seele*. A standard definition of soul reads something like: 'the spiritual or immaterial part of a human being or animal.' This essence is often thought to be immortal, and to survive death. The term is often applied to the essential life-force and personality of a living entity. This life-force is generally thought to be the consciousness and will of the individual, the thing that controls the body and makes it alive. The soul is usually thought to be immaterial, existing as a separate entity from the physical body and yet somehow fundamentally attached to it. The philosopher René Descartes (1596-1650) thought that the soul and body met at the the pineal gland, a small organ at the centre of the brain. While the soul is present within a body it can be said to animate, or give life to, that body, and when an entity dies its soul is thought to be released from the physical body.

What we are seeing here, in this confusion of closely related terms, is a manifestation of the difficulty we have in achieving a standard definition of consciousness, and what exactly constitutes human selfhood and personhood. This is a problem that continues to permeate contemporary approaches to the study of consciousness, a term which is similarly difficult to define in terms that are acceptable to everyone. We will return to the difficulties of defining consciousness in Chapter Three when we discuss consciousness in the context of shamanism and spirit possession.

For the purpose of clarity, I will use the terms 'spirit,' 'ghost' and 'soul' in slightly more specific ways. By doing so it is hoped that we can begin to understand more fully what we mean when we use them:

1. The *soul*, then, can be thought of as the life-force and personality of a person, or animal, while occupying a physical body.
2. The *spirit* can be thought of as the soul of a person freed from the limitations of the physical body, for example when the body dies, or as a soul that never occupied a body,
3. and a *ghost* may be thought of as a particular manifestation of a disembodied spirit.

Dividual Persons and Composite Souls

The category of the person has been of special interest to anthropologists. In particular, anthropologists are interested in the different ways by which persons are recognised and defined in different cultural contexts. Concepts of 'self' and 'person' are not, by any means, concrete in either psychology[29] or anthropology,[30] indeed categories of personhood are socially and culturally relative, varying widely across cultures.[31]

Anthropologist Marilyn Strathern, in thinking about Melanesian notions of the self, has highlighted two distinct categories which she has termed the *individual* and the *dividual* self. Strathern characterises the European notion of the self as individual in that Western Europeans generally tend to think of the self as a single and continuous stream of consciousness and personality that is independent of other consciousnesses. In other words the individual self is bounded. A dividual notion of the self, by contrast, is not bounded, it is not individual, but rather is porous and consists of multiple components. While the individual is self-centred and impermeable, the dividual is group-oriented and permeable.[32] A similar distinction can also be seen in different cultural notions of the soul. In European and American culture, the soul is generally thought of according to the Judeo-Christian notion of a single and unified centre of personality and consciousness:

an *individual* soul that persists after death and retains personal memories. However, as with so many other ideas in popular Western culture, the notion of a single unified soul is quite specific to Western culture and alternative conceptions, often consisting of multiple, or composite models of the soul, do exist in the belief systems of other cultures, past and present.

A fairly common notion in non-European belief systems is that the soul is made up of several, interrelated, component parts. The ancient Egyptian religious system contains a very good example of a composite model of personhood. According to ancient Egyptian belief every human being consists of five separate parts:

Part	Description	Function
Ib	The person's heart.	The seat of emotion.
Sheut	The person's shadow.	A person cannot exist without a shadow.
Ren	The person's name.	The person will live as long as their name is spoken.
Ba	The person's soul.	The individual personality. Can survive the death of the body.
Ka	The person's life-force and double.	The force that gives life to the person. The body dies when the *Ka* leaves.

All of these parts of the person are contained in the *khat*, the physical body. It is this belief in the mutual interconnectedness of various aspects of the soul that gives meaning to the ancient Egyptian practice of mummification, and their preoccupation with death and immortality. In ancient Egyptian belief the person's *Ka*, or life-force, existed as a double of their physical body and could continue to exist after death so long as the physical body remained intact. Mummification, therefore, sought to ensure that the physical body remained complete so that the *Ka* could continue to exist in the afterlife. The *Ba*, or the person's individual consciousness and personality, would then be able to occupy the *Ka*, the spiritual double of their physical body, and so continue to exist in Sekhet Aaru, the paradise of the afterlife.[33]

Similarly, the traditional Chinese conception of the soul is also a composite one, consisting of two separate parts, the *po* (associated with the yin), and the *hun* (associated with the yang). The *po* is the physical soul, and remains with the body at death, while the *hun* is the immaterial spiritual soul that leaves the body to dwell in the spirit realm. Sociologist Charles Emmons, in his study of Chinese spirit beliefs in the 1980s even found reference to belief in up to ten souls.[34]

Another example of a composite soul is found in the anthropologist Bronislaw Malinowski's examination of the spirit beliefs of the Trobriand Islanders of Kiriwina, in Papua New Guinea. Malinowski describes how, for the Islanders, at death the soul is believed to split into two parts: the *kosi* and the *baloma*. The *kosi* fulfills the role of what we might term a 'ghost' in that it haunts the gardens of the villagers, may be met while out walking along the road, or will knock on the doors of friends and relatives after the death of a person. Although, Malinowski writes, the villagers are afraid of encountering the *kosi*, they are not terrified in the way that Western ghost stories would lead us to expect, indeed the Trobriand Islanders treat the *kosi* as a sort of clown, or tricky prankster. After a few days the *kosi* is believed to dissipate, and will no longer cause problems for the villagers.

The second part of the soul, the *baloma*, however, takes on a more permanent existence in the afterlife as a spirit on the neighbouring island of Tuma. On the island the *baloma* grieves for those he has left behind before meeting with Topileta, the chief of the village of the dead. In order to be granted admission to the village of the dead the *baloma* must pay a fee to Topileta, and it is for this reason that the deceased person's body is buried alongside valuable grave goods, including ceremonial axes (*beku*) and jewels, which the *baloma* takes on its journey in their spiritual form.[35]

Spirit Worlds

Many of the world's cultures hold the belief that spirits inhabit an invisible spirit-world that exists in parallel with our own. Despite this apparent consensus, however, descriptions and models of the spirit world vary hugely from culture to culture. Nevertheless, there are also some surprising similarities between accounts, as the following two Native American descriptions demonstrate.

Anthropologist Gerald Weiss has described the Peruvian Campa universe as consisting of a series of layers arranged one above the other, each layer being inhabited by its own class of beings. For the inhabitants of each layer the world is perceived to be as solid underfoot as the Earth is to us. The Campa believe that their world is surrounded by spirits - their immediate neighbouring landscape, both visible and invisible, is populated by unseen entities. The good spirits have encampments on the mountain ridges of Campa territory, as well as in other layers of the universe. In the spirit world, the spirits live in their true forms, whether human or otherwise, and continue on with their lives in much the same way as the Campa themselves, except that the spirits need never want for anything and know nothing of illness, misery or death. While the spirits themselves are generally invisible to the lay person, shamans, owing to their special gifts, are able to perceive them both in the world of the living and during shamanic soul excursions to the spirit world (see Chapter Three for more on shamanism).[36]

The Swedish ethnographer Åke Hultkrantz also describes the North American Wind River Shoshoni universe as consisting of three levels: underground, ground and sky. These levels exist within a vertical hierarchy and are linked by an axis mundi, or world axis. Each world in the hierarchy is inhabited by various spirits: the sky is the domain of important spirits such as the Great Father, some air spirits, like Thunder, Lightning and Wind are closer to the earth which is home to the vast majority of spirits, including human beings. Water spirits and the Earth Mother inhabit the subterranean world.[37]

Belief in the existence of spirit-worlds parallel with the normal everyday world often form part of a particular culture's wider cosmology. It is important to note that these spirit worlds are not conceived as necessarily distant, or abstract, places, rather they are understood as immanent and present, overlaying, and influencing, the lived landscape.

Monotheism and Polytheism

Christianity, Judaism and Islam are good examples of monotheistic religions. This means that Christians, Jews and Muslims believe in a single God thought to be the creator of the universe. Polytheistic religions by contrast, such as Hinduism, Shinto, many contemporary traditional belief systems, and ancient religious systems like those of ancient Babylon, Greece and Egypt, hold that there are many gods, each with their own personalities, roles and motivations. We will begin with a brief exploration of how monotheistic religions conceive of the nature of God, before looking at polytheistic ideas.

According to Christianity, Judaism and Islam, three religions often referred to as the Abrahamic religions (because of their shared patriarch Abraham), God is conceived as a vast, often - though certainly not always - impersonal, creative intelligence. Typical descriptions of God include the notion that He is omnipresent (exists everywhere), omnipotent (all powerful), and omniscient (all knowing). As the creator of the universe, God is also thought to exist outside of time and space as a transcendent being. God is thought of as a first cause, and so, unlike a spirit, never occupied a physical body, and nor was He created by anything else, rather God is believed to have always existed. This is conception of God is often referred to as the 'God of Classical Theism.'

Unlike the notion of a single God held by the monotheistic Abrahamic religions, the gods of polytheistic religions are often described as anthropomorphic entities with desires and emotions similar to those of human beings. Unlike the Abrahamic God, polytheistic gods often have some form of creation story of their own, which explains how they came to be. According to ancient Greek mythology, for example, before the creation of the universe there existed a primordial void called Chaos from which the first gods, the Protogenoi, were born. These first gods, much like humans, mated with one another, thus creating more gods, until a whole pantheon (from the Greek words *pan* meaning 'all' and *-theios* meaning 'gods'), featuring several generations of related gods, came into existence.

It is worth noting at this point, however, that even the Christian God is often understood, and experienced, as a personal presence. Anthropologist Tanya Luhrmann, for example, describes the ways in which contemporary American Evangelical Christians form intensely personal relationships with God in an attempt to incorporate Him into their everyday lives.[38] Christian notions of the nature of God are further complicated by the Roman Catholic idea of the Holy Trinity - the father, the son and the Holy Ghost - a tripartite conception of God.[39]

Angels, Demons, Ancestors and Saints

Of course, believing in a single deity or a specific pantheon of deities does not exclude the possibility that there are other less powerful or intermediate spiritual beings. The Christian theological universe, for example, is also populated by angelic (good) and demonic (evil) beings that, although not partaking of the omnipotent nature of God, nevertheless possess supernatural attributes that elevate them above the human. These beings are believed to have been created by God, just as humans were. In a similar vein, the Islamic universe is also understood to be populated by Djinn (or genie), non-physical beings that are described in the Quran as one of three forms of sentient beings (including humans and angels) created by Allah. Djinn, like human beings, may be good, bad or neutral in temperament and possess free-will. Like humans, the djinn live in communities with rulers with their own traditions and social customs.

Many of the world's cultures hold ancestors, the spirits of deceased family members, in high regard. Even after death the ancestors continue to participate in everyday social life, often demanding attention and interaction.[40] In certain traditional forms of Chinese ancestor worship, for example, shrines, requiring regular offerings to the ancestors, are erected in the home serving as an everyday reminder of the presence of family spirits. In some traditions ancestor spirits may be transformed into fully fledged deities, thus blurring the distinction between ancestors and gods. A good example of such a tradition can be found in certain local Indian forms of Hindu folk belief, where small village cults are often established when an individual dies prematurely, violently or undeservedly.[41] This is similar in many ways to the transmutation of particularly pious folk into saints in Christianity, especially if they have been martyred in the name of their religion. Much like ancestor gods, Saints can be petitioned and asked for assistance by the living. Roman Catholicism and Orthodox Christianity have particularly rich traditions of Saint devotion, though they are not unique in this regard.

Other-Than-Human Persons, Relationships and Perspectivism

The category of 'other-than-human persons' has become quite popular in the anthropology of Native American cultures primarily because it helps to express the way in which Native American world-views relate to the living environment and the entities that inhabit and animate it, such as animals, plants, rocks, the weather, and so on. All of these are thought of as *persons*, like you or me, with consciousness, intentionality and agency all their own. From this perspective, living in the world necessarily entails the formation and maintenance of relationships with these non-human persons in order to live respectfully amongst the many being that surround and sustain us.[42] During his fieldwork amongst the Ojibwa people of North America, the ethnographer Irving Hallowell (1892-1974) noticed that the Ojibwa notion of personhood refers not only to human persons, but also to other entities, both physical and non-physical. The example he employed to highlight this idea, and to show just how ingrained this notion is within Ojibwa thought, culture and life, is in the use of the term 'grandfather,' which when used in the collective plural - as in 'our grandfathers' - is generally a referent for spiritual beings who are persons of a category *other than human.* Hallowell noted that that these other-than-human persons are not thought of in abstract terms, but rather are seen as active participants in the social group in much the same way as a 'real' grandfather might be. In other words, these other-than-human persons are just as real as everyday human persons.[43] A common belief found in many indigenous American cultures holds that personhood is relative. Just as we view ourselves as human beings - and categorise animals as animals, and plants as plants - the animals view themselves as human beings, and human beings as animals. This is a way of thinking about the world that anthropologists have labeled 'perspectivism.'[44]

Propitiating Spirits and Gods: Shrines and Offerings

All around the world, and all through time, cultures have sought to propitiate spirits and deities in a variety of different ways. The propitiation of spirits or deities often involves winning their favour, often by pleasing them in some way, for example by giving offerings of food and drink, or simply through recognising their presence. According to ancient Egyptian tradition, in order for the *Ka* to survive in the afterlife it was necessary for the living to provide it with a ready supply of food and drink for sustenance. To this end special 'false doors,' or 'Ka doors,' were constructed in tombs to enable the *Ka* to pass between the world of the dead and the world of the living. Offerings of food and drink would be left at these false doors, which were often inscribed with a special offering formula containing the name of the person to whom the offerings were intended. In a particularly striking example, in the tomb of a sixth dynasty official called Idu, the false door features a carved representation of the deceased with outstretched arms ready to receive the offerings that will sustain his *Ka* in the afterlife.[45]

In Mexico on the first and second days of November a great festival known as the Día de los Muertos (Day of the Dead) is held to commemorate and appease the spirits of the deceased. The roots of the festival can be traced back to the ancestor worship practiced by the indigenous peoples of central America, before the arrival of the Spanish in the sixteenth century, but today the festival owes just as much to the influence of Roman Catholicism, having merged with the Catholic celebrations of All Saints Day (November 1st) and All Souls Day (November 2nd). Over the course of the two-day festival people visit cemeteries to tidy the graves of their loved ones and construct small shrines to the memory of the deceased. Offerings of food, drink and flowers are left at the graves and shrines for the spirits, and the streets are decorated with brightly painted skulls (*calavera*). All of this is done in a carnival-like atmosphere of fun and frivolity with the aim of remembering the good times when deceased loved ones were still alive.[46]

Just as with the Ancient Egyptian *Ka*, the Chinese notion of the *po* (the spiritual component of the soul), also requires sustenance in the form of offerings if it is to thrive in the spirit world. The traditional Chinese Hungry Ghost Festival (*Yu Lan*) is a month-long celebration, beginning at the start of the seventh lunar month, during which the spirits of deceased ancestors are believed to be freed from the realm of the dead by King Yama, a god of death, to visit the living. As with the Mexican Day of the Dead, offerings of food and drink are laid out for the spirits in shrines. Offerings are also made in the form of burning small piles of 'Hell Notes,' a kind of money made from joss paper produced especially for offering to the ancestors, who use its spiritual essence.[47]

It would appear that the belief that spirits simply want to be remembered is a fairly common cross-cultural trait, and that if they are not remembered, or honoured in the correct way, they may become angry and bring bad luck to the living.

Representing Supernatural Beings

Because spirits and gods are often conceived as invisible beings, many of the world's cultures have developed different ways of representing spirits and gods in the physical world. One of these ways is through performance and spirit possession rituals, and these will be discussed in Chapter Three. Another way is through physical objects and artistic representation. Fetishism is a term that refers to the belief that certain objects possess supernatural power, and is a useful concept for thinking about the representation of supernatural beings. For many, the physical representation of spirits in statues is equated with the creation of a physical body for immaterial spirits to inhabit. The worship of physical representations of spirits and deities plays a central role in popular Chinese religion, for example. Indeed, statues and images are often taken not as simple representations, but rather as the actual physical embodiment of deities - as bodies for the gods. These bodies are interacted with in much the same way as human-to-human interactions, providing worshippers with direct, physical, access to the deities they worship. In popular Chinese religion, therefore, the representation of spirits and deities in statues and artwork is an act of materialisation.[48]

Supernatural Encounters

So far we have dealt mainly with belief systems, but there is another side to this story that cannot be ignored, and that is the experiences people claim to have with what we might term spirits, demons and gods. This section will explore some of the different ways in which the experience of such entities is described and interpreted in different cultural traditions.

Ghosts and Spirits

As we have seen, E.B. Tylor attributed the belief in supernatural beings to misinterpreting encounters with people in dreams as real experiences. Indeed, many cultural traditions do hold that it is possible to make contact with ancestors and other spirits while in the dream state. Amongst the Islanders of Kiriwina, Papua New Guinea, villagers, especially women, are often said to be visited by the *baloma* in dreams. The following account of what parapsychologists would call a 'crisis-apparition' was documented by Bronislaw Malinowski while conducting fieldwork on the Trobriand Islands during the First World War:

> One night Kalohusa dreamt that his mother, an old woman...came to him and told him that she had died. He was very sad, and apparently showed his grief by wailing...All the others knew that "something must have happened in Omarkana." When they learned on their way home that the mother of Gumigawa'ia had died, they were not at all astonished, and found in this the explanation of Kalohusa's dream.

Dreams are not, however, the only means by which spirits and gods are encountered. Spontaneous waking meetings are just as likely to occur. Malinowski also describes encounters with the baloma while awake, for example:

> One day he (Bagido'u) was getting water our of a well in the raiboag (stony woodland) on Tuma (the Island of the dead), when a baloma hit him on the back, and, on turning round, Bagido'u just saw a shadow retreating into the bush.[49]

This particular account accords well with the European poltergeist (from the German for 'noisy ghost'), which is often characterised as a spirit capable of affecting the physical environment (we will hear more about poltergeists in Chapter Six). Although these two accounts are take from a single cultural context, they are representative, more generally, of the forms in which ghosts and spirits are usually experienced - as apparitions, or as physical phenomena.

Extraterrestrial Encounters, Marian Apparitions, Fairy-Folk and Psychedelic Entities

A particular kind of supernatural encounter that has become increasingly common in the Western world is the so-called Alien Abduction experience, in which an individual has the experience of being taken aboard an alien space craft, often under coercion, where they are then subjected to some form of medical examination. The key elements in this narrative structure involve:

1) Capture: Strange beings seize and take the witness aboard a UFO.
2) Examination: These beings subject the witness to a physical and mental examination.

3) Conference: A conversation with the beings follows.

4) Tour: The beings show their captive around the ship.

5) Otherworldly Journey: The ship flies the witness to some strange and unearthly place.

6) Theophany: An encounter with a divine being occurs.

7) Return: The witness comes back to Earth, leaves the ship, and re-enters normal life.

8) Aftermath: Physical, mental and paranormal aftereffects continue in the wake of the abduction.

Folklorist Thomas Bullard has noted distinct similarities between the narrative structure of such experiences and that of more traditional supernatural kidnap narratives involving fairies.[50] Similarly, Peter Rojcewicz has suggested that alien abductions exist within a continuum of extraordinary encounters, including encounters with other creatures from folklore and myth, such as angels, fairies, and other monsters. Rojcewicz further suggests that these encounters represent instances of human confrontation with the anomalous, which are subsequently shaped according to cultural expectation.[51] The UFOlogist Jacques Vallee has made similar suggestions about the UFO phenomenon and its relation to older supernatural entity encounters.[52] The implication of this research is that there is a fairly standard common core to such experiences, with differences emerging as products of cultural interpretation.

Such encounters are similar, in certain respects, to the visions of the Virgin Mary, often referred to as Marian apparitions, which are alleged to have appeared before a 14 year-old shepherdess called Bernadette Soubirous at Lourdes in France. On Thursday 11th February 1858 Bernadette was collecting firewood by a small stream when she heard a gust of wind that directed her attention towards a small grotto in which she saw a young lady dressed in white with a blue belt and golden roses on her feet. Bernadette recited the Rosary with the mysterious woman who promptly disappeared once the recitation was over. This was the first of eighteen encounters between Bernadette and the Blessed Virgin Mary, and was the event that transformed the small town of Lourdes into a thriving centre of international pilgrimage.[53]

Encounters with apparently sentient entities while under the influence of psychoactive substances are well documented in the psychedelic literature. Terence McKenna, in his 1975 book *The Invisible Landscape*, described his encounters with weird insectoid entities during an ayahuasca trip in the amazon jungle. Countless people have recorded their experiences of a distinctively feminine presence while smoking *Salvia divinorum*, a herb traditionally used to divinatory practices.[54] Rick Strassman's famous 2001 book *DMT: The Spirit Molecule* contains numerous references to meetings with insect-like and extraterrestrial beings after receiving intravenous doses of the highly psychoactive compound DMT under laboratory conditions.[55] In his autobiographical book *Cosmic Trigger*, counter-cultural philosopher Robert Anton Wilson (1932-2007) described an encounter with a dancing 'man with warty green skin and pointy ears' following a peyote trip,[56] likening it to Carlos Castaneda's (1925-1998) peyote encounter with the spirit Mescalito, as described in *The Teachings of Don Juan*.[57] More recently parapsychologist David Luke has described numerous meetings with 'thousand eyed' sentient beings after smoking DMT.[58] Such encounters give a clear indication of the central role played by altered states of consciousness in the experience of spiritual entities.

How Long Have People Believed in Supernatural Beings?

Attempting to uncover the beliefs of our ancestors is a particularly difficult task. Archaeological evidence, especially prehistoric data - which by definition completely lacks historical documentation - is particularly difficult to interpret. Because archaeologists must rely solely on material remains - such as bones, pottery and other artificial objects - it is very difficult to gain an appreciation of the thoughts, feelings and beliefs of the long gone societies that created such objects. Imagine, for example, trying to decipher the meaning and purpose of a church, with all of its elaborate symbolism, without the benefit of historical written sources to give an idea of the system of thought and belief underlying its construction. It would be extremely difficult, if not impossible, to gain a complete picture of the beliefs that inspired the material remains. This is the difficulty faced by archaeologists when trying to work out what people believed by looking only at the objects and structures they left behind. Nevertheless, there are certain clues that can help to elucidate these questions.

Archaeologists have looked to the deliberate burial of the dead as evidence for the early development of religious thought in human beings. The act of intentionally burying the dead has been interpreted as indicating a concern for an aspect of the deceased that survives the death of the physical body, especially when the burial is associated with grave goods and other deliberately placed objects.[59] The earliest instances of intentional burial so far discovered date back about 130,000 years to the Upper Palaeolithic period, and were excavated in the Skhūl cave system in Qafzeh, Israel. The graves at Qafzeh contain seven adults and three children, whose skeletal remains display a mixture of physical characteristics associated with modern humans and Neanderthals, though they are now generally thought to be archaic modern humans. Several of the burials at Qafzeh are also associated with grave goods, possibly indicating a conception of some form of surviving spirit or soul. The burials with grave goods contained collections of shells not found in the local area, perhaps suggesting that they were used as decorative beads, maybe possessing an emotional or symbolic significance to the deceased. Another individual at Qafzeh was buried with the jaw bone of a boar. The body of a boy aged about thirteen years, and clutching Red Deer antlers in his hands, was also uncovered in the cave.[60] Although this evidence does not necessarily imply that the Palaeolithic folk of Qafzeh believed in the existence of spirits or souls, it does suggest some form of thought beyond the confines of the purely physical, even at this early stage in the development of modern humans. One thing that is for sure, however, is that from the upper Palaeolithic period onwards modern human beings, as they spread throughout Africa, Europe, Asia, Australasia and the Americas, began to develop increasingly complex systems of belief that were vividly expressed in material culture, and as the millennia progressed the evidence for spiritual beliefs began to proliferate.

We will now skip forward several thousand years (but still remaining firmly within the Upper Palaeolithic period), from the burials at Qafzeh to the painted caves of Lascaux in France to consider some of the most exciting expressions of prehistoric thought. The caves at Lascaux are home to over two thousand images painted directly onto the rock surface some 17,300 years ago. Deep inside the caves the walls are adorned with colourful representations of horses, stags and bison, amongst other large animals. Dotted amongst these naturalistic depictions of large herd animals can be found numerous geometric patterns. Once again, it is particularly difficult to know what these paintings meant to those who created them, but numerous interpretations have been put forward. One theory of particular interest to us, with regard to the light it might shed on the history of belief in spirits, is that proposed by the anthropologist David Lewis-Williams, who concludes that the paintings possessed a spiritual, or religious, significance to their makers. Drawing on similarities between the unusual geometric forms dotted around the Lascaux caves and similar motifs in the rock art of the San Bushmen of the Kalahari, Lewis-Williams suggests that the Lascaux paintings are visual representations of experiences during altered states of consciousness (see Chapter Three for a fuller discussion of ASCs). If this is indeed the case, the paintings at Lascaux may be shamanic in nature, depicting sacred spirit-animals, with the caves themselves serving as a gateway into the spirit-world and suggest a particularly early origin for belief in supernatural beings.[61]

Theories

The main anthropological theories of supernatural beings can broadly be classified as social theories, psychological theories and cognitive theories:

Social theories hold that supernatural beings are social constructs: produced by society for the benefit of society. As we have already seen, Émile Durkheim thought of supernatural beings as nothing more than socially constructed focal points for societies to worship. Worshipping a particular pantheon of supernatural beings, for instance, gives a society a common ideal and sense of identity, which in turn increases the solidarity of the group. While social models such as this make sense when it comes to thinking about large, relatively impersonal entities, but begs the question as to why beliefs in less widespread entities develop, especially, as in the case of alien abductees, when such beliefs lead to social marginalisation.

Psychological theories suggest that belief in the existence of supernatural beings is the result of the human need for stability in a transient and unpredictable world. Supernatural beings provide explanations for natural events, illness, fortune and misfortune. In other words, they represent an explanatory framework for dealing with uncertainties. In a similar vein, *cognitive theories* suggest that supernatural beings are the product of misinterpreted, or misunderstood, cognitive processes. A good example would be the human propensity to see faces in clouds. As already noted, cognitive anthropologist Stewart Guthrie has suggested that belief in supernatural beings arises from a failure to understand that such processes are hardwired into our brains (perhaps as by-products of natural selection), and that such observations do not mean that there are actual entities out there in objective reality.

The experiential source hypothesis, as expounded by David Hufford in his study of the Old Hag tradition of Newfoundland, by contrast, suggests that belief in supernatural beings arises from direct personal experiences. As a phenomenological approach the experiential source hypothesis does not take a definitive position with regard to the reality of the supernatural beings encountered: it does not suggest that the beings encountered are necessarily grounded in what might be termed a 'supernatural reality,' but neither does it suggest that all such experiences are the product of hallucination, illness or misinterpretation. What the experiential source hypothesis suggests is that we must take experiential claims seriously in and of themselves.

CHAPTER 3

SHAMANISM AND SPIRIT POSSESSION

~

S hamanism has captured the popular imagination since the seventeenth century when explorers, returning home from their adventures in remote regions of the world, first began to relate their encounters with mysterious characters who claimed to leave their bodies and fly to the spirit-world while experiencing ecstatic trance states. Similarly, the idea of possession by spirits has always been a subject of fascination for the Western mind, and is perhaps best represented nowadays by our preoccupation with films such as *The Exorcist* - and the many imitations it has spawned - which deals specifically with possession by demonic forces. But what do we actually know about shamanism and spirit possession as distinct from the notions prevalent in popular culture? This chapter will give an introduction to these fascinating social and psychological phenomena.

What are Altered States of Consciousness?

We will come across the notion of altered states of consciousness (ASCs) at numerous points throughout this chapter, as well as the chapters that follow on from it, so it seems reasonable to begin our discussion of shamanism and spirit possession with a brief exploration of what they are. First of all it is necessary to define what we are mean when we use the word 'consciousness.'

Consciousness is a tricky term to define primarily because science does not yet fully understand what it is, or how it arises.[62] A simple starting point for this discussion, however, is to suggest that consciousness is our subjective sense of perception - how we experience the world around us, and our sense of self awareness. It is this aspect of consciousness, the fact that we experience at all, that is the great mystery facing those who wish to understand consciousness.[63] We do not, as of yet, understand how self-aware consciousness (as we all experience every day) can emerge from physical matter (from which our bodies are made). Philosopher David Chalmers has referred to this as the hard problem of consciousness. Indeed it is such a hard problem that debates are still raging between philosophers, psychologists, biologists and physicists about what exactly consciousness consists of and how it arises, or indeed whether it exists at all.

With this confusing state of affairs in mind, then, altered states of consciousness may be thought of as ways of experiencing the world and our sense of self that are different to the way in which we have such experiences in our normal, everyday, waking state. A good example of an altered state of consciousness that we all experience on a fairly regular basis is the dream state. In the dream state our experience is often radically different to the way in which we experience the world in the waking state, and this is only one of numerous other states of consciousness that we have the capacity to experience.

Altered states of consciousness can be brought about in many ways. Some, like dreaming, occur naturally as a normal function of everyday life, while others may be deliberately induced through a variety of different techniques. Throughout the world human beings employ countless methods of consciousness alteration as part of their religious and spiritual practices. Meditation and prayer, processes involving relaxation and introspection, are common techniques in many religious traditions including Buddhism, Hinduism, Christianity, Judaism and Islam, amongst others. Many traditions utilise repetitious rhythms and dancing as a means to induce altered states of consciousness, such as the dancing of Candomblé spirit mediums in Brazil or the whirling dervishes of Sufi Islam. Yet other traditions employ various psychoactive drugs to cause changes in consciousness, and have done for many thousands of years,[64] for example the use of cannabis in certain Hindu Brahmin sects and in Rastafarianism, where it is used as an aid to Bible study, and the consumption of the hallucinogenic peyote cactus amongst the Huichol people of Central America. Other techniques of consciousness alteration include sensory deprivation (to reduce sensory input and stimulate mental imagery) and sensory overload (to hyper-stimulate the brain). Fasting and intense physical ordeals are also employed, in one form or another, to enter into altered states across the globe.

Anthropologist Erika Bourguignon (1924-2015) conducted a cross-cultural study of 488 societies across the globe and discovered that ninety percent of her sample featured some form of institutionalised altered state of consciousness. The majority of the world's cultures therefore possess the belief that altered states of consciousness have the capacity to put the experiencer in contact with a sacred and transcendent world, and so they are frequently treated with great respect.[65] Anthropologist Charles Laughlin has separated different cultural attitudes towards altered states of consciousness into two broad categories:

Monophasic cultures, which would be exemplified by mainstream Euro-American culture, place a particular emphasis on just one state of consciousness - everyday "normal" waking consciousness. Such cultures consider waking consciousness to be the dominant, most practical and productive, form of consciousness, and generally hold altered states to be inferior and impractical. *Polyphasic* cultures, by contrast, possess an appreciation of a variety of different states of consciousness, and an understanding that different states might be useful for different tasks. For example dream states, or states induced by the consumption of psychoactive drugs, may be held in high regard as means of gaining useful information and access to spiritual realms.[66]

As an illustration, amongst the Yanomami Indians of the Orinoco Valley in Venezuela a psychoactive snuff called *Epena* or *Yopo*, made from the roasted and ground beans of the Anadenanthera peregrina tree, is used to initiate contact with the invisible world of spirits as well as for ritual healing purposes.[67] Similarly, when the psychoactive drink ayahuasca, consisting of stewed Banisteriopsis caapi vines and leaves containing the highly psychoactive compound DMT, is consumed in the Ecuadorian and Peruvian rainforest the spirit-world is said to become visible to the experiencer. In a completely different context, Muslim Sufi mystics claim that the altered states of consciousness experienced during whirling dervishes are a form of religious ecstasy that brings them closer to Allah. It is clear to see, as Bourguignon's research suggested, that altered states of consciousness are almost universally associated with the sacred. This chapter will deal specifically with two distinct (but overlapping) applications of altered states of consciousness to access information from the spiritual realm: shamanism and spirit possession.

What is Shamanism?

The word 'shaman' is an anglicized form of the Siberian Tungus and Evenki term *šamán*, which is used to refer to a particular type of religious practitioner whose primary role is as a mediator between the world of human beings and the world of spirits. Because of the very specific cultural context of the term, some commentators have suggested that the label of 'shaman' should only really be applied to the practices of the arctic, and that other local terms ought to be used in reference to the practices of people outside of this region. Nevertheless, the term is widely used by anthropologists to refer to similar practices around the world, especially practices in which the practitioner is believed to travel to the world of spirits. Indeed, the historian of religion Mircea Eliade (1907-1986) defined shamanism generally as a 'technique of ecstasy,'[68] shamanism is not, therefore, defined by a specific doctrine (as other religions are), but rather by the methods it employs. Practices labelled as shamanism are found on practically every continent and generally partake of some, or all, of the following distinctive characteristics:

1. The belief that the shaman travels to the spirit-world to retrieve information or to rescue lost souls.
2. The use of altered states of consciousness to access the world of spirits.
3. The ability of the shaman to heal the sick.
4. The ability of the shaman to transform into non-human forms, such as animals.

How Old is Shamanism?

Many commentators have suggested that shamanism represents the world's oldest system of religious belief and practice. As has already been noted though the term 'shamanism' does not refer to a single body of beliefs but rather to particular practices and techniques employed across the world, so it is particularly difficult to determine how long people have been shamanising based on physical archaeological evidence. There are some clues, however, that suggest a very early beginning for shamanism. It has been argued that the cave paintings of the Palaeolithic period, such as those at Lascaux in France, represent expressions of an early shamanic world-view, suggesting that shamanic practices could date as least as far back as 18,000 years ago. An image of a human figure lying flat on the ground, and apparently wearing a bird-shaped mask, and images of half-human-half-animal figures referred to as therianthropes, have been particularly tantalising to those wishing to interpret the paintings at Lascaux as evidence of Palaeolithic shamanism.[69]

Biography of the Shaman

It has been widely noted by scholars that shamans are often initiated into their career as healer and mediator between the worlds following a serious illness or life-crisis during which they are singled out by the spirits to perform this important role for their community. The illness and recovery are symbolic of the death and rebirth of the shaman. As one who has died and been reborn the shaman is able to mediate between the world of human beings and the world of spirits. The following account, given by an Oroqen shaman called Chuonnasuan from Northern China, is a good example of such an initiatory illness experience. At the age of sixteen Chuonnasuan fell ill after the unexpected death of his brother. As the illness worsened, Chuonnasuan's mother decided to take him to a local shaman called Wuliyen who agreed to conduct a healing ritual for the boy because the spirits had evidently selected him for shamanic training. For three whole nights of intensive ritual activity in a large yurt, during which offerings of moose, duck, goose, fish and antelope were given to the spirits, Wuliyen sang songs and beat her shaman's drum over the boy and introduced him to over fifty spirits who possessed him and taught him how to perform sacred dances. At the end of the ceremony Chuonnasuan emerged cured from the yurt, ready to pursue his own career as a shaman.[70]

For some, shamanism is the traditional vocation of a particular family lineage and will be handed down from generation to generation, while for others the calling comes in the form of a dream or initiatory experience. Amongst the Yanomami Indians of the Orinoco Valley in Venezuela the *shapori* (shamanic practitioner) initiation involves the ritual consumption of the psychoactive snuff Yopo, which is understood to be both the food of the spirits and the means by which the *shapori* is able to contact the spirit-world. The Yanomamo name for the shamanic initiation, *hekura prai*, essentially translates as the 'metamorphosis of a human being into a hekura spirit.' Following initiation, therefore, the shaman is believed to have become one with the spirits - the body has been transformed into a spirit body. Over the course of the initiation ceremony the neophyte, while under the influence of the *yopo* snuff, experiences the occupation of his body by numerous *hekura* spirits that proceed to dismember him with machetes and pierce him with arrows. Through this process, much as in the case of shamanic sickness discussed above, the initiate experiences death and rebirth. He is reconstructed as a living embodiment of the *hekura* with new spirit allies who will aid him in the future. This theme of dismemberment and reconstruction by the spirits is particularly common in shamanic initiation narratives in many different cultural settings.[71]

Shamanism and Performance

The influential structuralist anthropologist Claude Levi-Strauss' discussion of the Native American Kwakiutl medicine man Quesalid - who was interviewed by the ethnologist Franz Boas (1858-1942) in the 1920s - provides a good example of the kind of techniques employed by shamans in their healing rituals. Quesalid was a trainee shaman who did not believe in the power of his teachers, and thought their practices were simply deliberate acts of fraud with no benefit to the person in need of healing. Nevertheless, in being initiated into the secrets of his teachers, Quesalid learned their healing techniques, which consisted of a mixture of pantomime, sleight of hand, techniques for inducing vomiting, simulation of fainting and fits, and the singing of sacred songs. Suffice to say that Quesalid was not impressed by the techniques he was learning. Before he had a chance to abandon his apprenticeship for a more straight forward career, however, Quesalid was summoned to treat a sick person who had dreamed of him as their healer. Quesalid agreed to treat the sick person, and despite his doubts about the efficacy of the techniques he had learned, his treatment was successful and the sick person was soon healed. Because of such successes Quesalid became widely known as a powerful healer and came to consider the methods he had learned to be superior to those of other shamans. His performances, despite consisting of deliberate acts of trickery and deception, were nevertheless entirely effective cures of illness and go a long way towards demonstrating the complex relationship between performance, consciousness and the body. Although Quesalid was essentially performing tricks, and so deceiving his patients, his cures worked and as such surely cannot be interpreted as fraudulent.[72]

Shamanism and Psychoactive Drugs

As we have already seen, many commentators have argued that shamanism is, strictly speaking, a Siberian phenomenon, and that the term should not be used outside of this context. In traditional Siberian Tungus shamanism, the shaman employs repetitious drum rhythms in order to achieve an altered state of consciousness conducive to entering into the spirit world. This observation led certain researchers, most notably Mircea Eliade, to conclude that other techniques of consciousness alteration, in particular the use of psychoactive drugs, represent degenerate forms of shamanism. This assertion, however, has not gone un-criticised. Many anthropologists working in the field have observed practices very much like those of Tungus shamans, performing the same essential community roles (healer, psychopomp, and mediator between the human and spirit worlds, and so on), but utilising psychoactive drugs as a means to access the spirit world.[73]

Contemporary Neo-Shamanism

In recent years shamanism has experienced a resurgence in popular interest in the Euro-American world. This growth of interest was inspired to a great extent by the exceedingly popular books of Carlos Castaneda (1925-1998), which captured the popular imagination in the late 1960s and early 1970s with his tales of initiation into ancient Native American mysteries. Although there is considerable debate as to whether Castaneda's books represent factual or fictional accounts of his apprenticeship to a Yaqui sorcerer named Don Juan (note that Castaneda's book are not actually about shamanism), they undoubtedly had a significant effect on popular attitudes towards traditional systems of belief, and certainly inspired many to pursue an interest in learning about shamanic, and other consciousness altering techniques.

The writings of anthropologist Michael Harner (1929-2018), who conducted fieldwork in the late 1950s amongst the Shuar people of the Ecuadorian Amazon, have also been hugely influential in the development of modern Euro-American Neo-Shamanic movements. Based on cross-cultural research into shamanic traditions, Harner developed what he called 'core shamanism'; a distillation and simplification of various shamanic techniques. Today, core shamanism is one of the most popular Neo-Shamanic movements, with many thousands of practitioners attesting to the efficacy of its techniques.[74]

As one would expect, there has also been a great deal of debate as to whether modern Neo-Shamanic movements, like core shamanism, can really be categorised together with the more traditional shamanic systems. This issue really comes back to the old argument amongst scholars and anthropologists as to the definition of shamanism: should shamanism be defined in terms of specific cultural manifestations, with different names for different traditions, or according to the techniques employed and the types of experience described by practitioners? Ultimately, this is simply a matter of personal scholarly preference.

Theories of Shamanism

Classical theories of shamanism often concluded that shamans were essentially suffering from various types of neurosis. Early ethnographer's such as Paul Radin (1883-1959), for example, characterised Eskimo shamanic practitioners as being of the 'neurotic-epileptoid type,' and George Devereux (1908-1985) argued that the shaman was 'psychiatrically a genuinely ill person.' More recently, however, psychiatrist Wolfgang Jilek has criticised such approaches as distinct manifestations of what he calls a 'eurocentric and positivistic fallacy' that misinterprets the significance and role of altered states of consciousness in other cultures, treating them as psychopathological in nature (see discussion of monophasic and polyphasic cultures above).[75] Indeed, historian Ronald Hutton has suggested that shamanism represents precisely the kind of phenomenon that modern - Euro-American - rationalist culture developed in opposition to, so it is quite unsurprising that Euro-American commentators should so grossly misinterpret shamanic practices.[76] Some of the most promising recent theories of shamanism emphasise its therapeutic efficacy, and suggest that it likely emerged as an early form of medicine and psychotherapy. Sociologist James McClenon, for example, has put forward the 'ritual healing hypothesis,' in which he argues that shamanic rituals function through a combination of hypnotizability on behalf of the patient and the placebo effect, and that they have served an evolutionary function in curing certain illnesses.[77] Similarly, Michael Winkelman has argued in favour of treating shamanism as a highly evolved biopsychosocial capacity, with clear benefits for adaptation and survival in our species.[78] Such approaches highlight the holistic nature of shamanism, combining perspectives on consciousness, the body, society and culture.

What is Spirit Possession?

Spirit possession can be simply defined as the belief that certain individuals, during particular states of consciousness, surrender the command of their bodies to an external intelligence which then controls that body as though it was its own.[79] Broadly speaking spirit possession can be split into two distinct categories, the first being spontaneous, or involuntary possession, whereby an intruding spirit takes control of an individual's body without that person's consent, and the second being voluntary possession, often referred to as spirit mediumship, whereby the possessed deliberately invokes a state of possession and wilfully surrenders control of his/her body to an external intelligence. As with shamanism, belief in spirit possession, both voluntary and involuntary, is a worldwide phenomenon. Anthropologist Erika Bourguignon's already mentioned study of altered states found that seventy percent of her sample of 488 societies associated such states with the notion of spirit possession, giving a total of over three hundred of the world's societies who practice a culturally recognised form of spirit possession.

Popular portrayals of spirit possession, such as those found in literature, film and television, generally give the impression that people are only ever possessed by evil entities, demons or the Devil. It should be noted, however, that this portrayal is particular to Judeo-Christian notions of spirit possession as the work of the Devil, or lesser demonic entities. Although possession by evil spirits does occur in other traditions, usually requiring some form of exorcism (the ritual eviction of an intruding spirit from the body of an afflicted individual), it is generally in the context of spontaneous, or involuntary, pathological possession, whereby illnesses are interpreted as the direct result of possession by malevolent entities.[81]

Much more commonly spirit possession, as a deliberate and voluntary practice, involves the incorporation of benevolent gods, nature spirits or ancestor spirits. Voluntary forms of spirit possession are often referred to as 'mediumship.' For example, in the Afro-Brazilian religions of Umbanda and Candomblé mediums enter into trance states while dancing furiously to repetitive drum rhythms in order to incorporate gods known as Orixas, each with their own distinctive dances and characteristics, and in the modern European Spiritualist and Brazilian Spiritist traditions the spirits of the dead may be embodied for the positive task of healing the sick.[82] Amongst the Nayaka people of southern India spirit mediums are voluntarily possessed by nature spirits called devara,[83] while on the Island of Ternate in Indonesia mediums incorporate ancestral spirits to be consulted on important political issues.[84] Spirit possession is, therefore, a much more complex phenomenon than its representation in the popular media suggests.

Spirit Possession and Shamanism

As we have already seen, spirit possession and shamanism are both practices that employ altered states of consciousness as a means of providing a link between the human and spiritual worlds. There are, however, significant differences between the two practices. Chief amongst these differences is the relationship between the medium/shaman and the spirits. Historian of Religion Mircea Eliade, for instance, differentiated between spirit possession and shamanism on the grounds that 'the shaman controls his 'spirits' in the sense that he, a human being, is able to communicate with the dead, 'demons', and 'nature spirits', without...becoming their instrument.'[85] The medium, by contrast, is understood to surrender his/her control of the body to an external intelligence, while the shaman remains in complete control during his performance. While mediums often report amnesia after their trance performances, the shaman is able to fully recall his trance journeys through the spirit worlds. It is for this reason that Eliade considered shamanism a more developed practice than mediumship and possession.

Although it is easy, and often useful, to make clear-cut distinctions like this in theory, the real life ethnographic data do not always fit so neatly into such rigidly defined categories, and aspects of mediumship and shamanism very often overlap with one another. Anthropologist

Zeljko Jokic, for example, describes how in contemporary Siberian Buriyat Neo-Shamanism shamanic performances partake of a character very much like spirit possession, with the shamans unable to fully recall their experiences in the spirit world. Jokic explains this by recourse to the fact that Buriyat shamanism was outlawed during the Soviet period, so the shamans reviving their tradition today must now learn their practices from scratch, and as such are not currently proficient in controlling the shamanic trance.[86] Mediumship - whereby spirits occupy the body of the medium - is often also a technique in the wider repertoire of the shaman, and Euro-American platform (clairvoyant) mediums do not necessarily lose consciousness or display alterations of personality when receiving and giving messages from the spirit world, thus suggesting an experience somewhat more akin to the shamanic trance journey than possession.

Spirit Possession and Performance

In many nonwestern societies, as well as in Euro-American traditions, a particular spirit or deity, when incorporated during spirit possession demonstrations, is discerned through specific socially and culturally recognised behaviours. In this respect, therefore, spirit possession can be thought of in terms of a performance. For example, Paul Stoller describes how the spirits incorporated by West African Songhay spirit mediums 'assume ritualized postures and vocalize in ways characteristic of their families, which marks their powerful otherness.'[87] Amongst the Kel Ewey Tuareg of Niger, women's trance performances involve a head dance known as *asul* which features 'sideways movement of the head and neck, gradually becoming more vigorous and including the shoulders and torso.'[88] As a further example, in the Afro-Brazilian religion of Batuque a medium must act in certain ways while possessed if they are to be perceived as genuinely under the influence of a spirit. Anthropologists Seth and Ruth Leacock explain how 'in order to prove that an *encantado* is really present, the medium must dance, sing the proper songs, and interact with the other participants in the ceremony in an acceptable manner.'[89]

Considering spirit possession practices as performances, however, does not mean that such practices are in any sense 'fake' or delusional products of fantasy.[90] Rather, performance can be thought of as an essential technique in the manifestation of spiritual entities. Indeed,

41

performance theorist Richard Schechner has suggested that, when considering such performances, anthropologists should attempt to enter into an alternative mode of understanding performance - not simply as an 'act' or as 'pretending,' but as an actual transformation of the performer's body.[91] In other words, the medium *becomes* the spirit or deity when possessed. Similarly, emphasising the role of performance in spirit possession does not deny the importance of the psychological and neurophysiological processes that underlie the trance state, and nor does it necessarily detract from the importance of the medium's subjective experiences while in the trance state.

Theories of Spirit Possession

For as long as anthropologists have been describing spirit possession practices in the field, they have also tried to explain them using various theoretical models. This last section will give a brief overview of some of the different explanations offered by anthropologists for spirit possession practices throughout the world. The earliest anthropologists looked at the often erratic behaviour of people claiming to be possessed by spirits (their vigorous dancing, uncontrollable twitches and apparent insensibility to the world around them when in trance), and likened them to neurological conditions such as epilepsy and hysteria. The nineteenth century sociologist Herbert Spencer (1820-1903), for example, explained spirit possession beliefs as 'primitive' theories of epilepsy, whereby the true underlying neurological cause of epilepsy - which Spencer though would only be revealed by materialist science - was misdiagnosed as the influence of supernatural beings.[92] This association of spirit possession with illness has been particularly popular in anthropology, and continues to this day.

A parallel is often drawn between spirit possession and other pathological conditions such as dissociative identity disorder (DID), a condition that used to be called multiple personality disorder (MPD). Put simply, dissociation is a state in which an individual experiences a partial or total disconnection between their sense of self (including memories and experiences), and their actions. Someone who suffers from dissociative identity disorder, then, experiences a dissociative state during which their identity is apparently replaced by another personality - or many personalities -with its own memories and distinctive behaviours. Once the individual returns from his/her dissociative state they have no recollection of their actions during the preceding interval. The similarities between dissociative identity disorder and spirit possession are clearly very striking.[93]

Nevertheless, there are significant differences in terms of the neurological activity of people suffering from conditions such as epilepsy and DID and those experiencing spirit possession. Recent studies using portable EEG (electroencephalograph) devices (which measure the electrical activity of the brain using electrodes attached to the scalp), to examine Balinese trance dancers, have shown that the EEG patterns of possessed trance dancers are different to those of individuals suffering from such conditions as epilepsy, schizophrenia and dissociative identity disorder. However, the EEG recordings did measure unusual activity in the brain during the trance performance, revealing heightened activity in the theta (associated with relaxed wakefulness and REM sleep) and alpha (associated with relaxation, and generally occurring when the eyes are closed) frequency waves, thus indicating, at the very least, a neurophysiological basis for the spirit possession experience.[94]

Anthropologist Morton Klass (1927-2000) sought to distinguish spirit possession from dissociative identity disorder by focusing on the wider cultural recognition and acceptance of the behaviours and alternate identities expressed in possession practices. According to Klass, a disorder by definition requires that the behaviours exhibited contravene social norms and so cause a disruption to the individual's normal functioning in society. In most societies where spirit possession is practiced, however, the behaviours exhibited by the possessed are certainly not in contravention to social norms, indeed they are expected as a part of the possession performance. The same critique can be applied to the entities incorporated during the possession performance; while in dissociative identity disorder the alternate personalities cause a disturbance to the individual's daily life, thus impairing their normal social functioning, during spirit possession rituals the entities are expected and desired, and often have a much wider cultural significance (for example in the incorporation of deities). It is for this reason that Klass coined the term patterned dissociative identity to refer to spirit possession. Spirit possession differs from dissociative identity disorder, therefore, in that it adheres to socially recognised patterns of behaviour expectation.[95]

Further reasons to question the classification of spirit possession as a symptom of underlying disorder or illness include the notion that, in many societies, the ability to become possessed by a spirit is perceived as a positive and desirable skill. In some societies the ability to incorporate spiritual beings serves to improve the social status of the individual. For example, amongst the Ga in Ghana the ability to incorporate spirits provides women with significant social benefits. The Ga believe that the relationship between the medium and the deity she incorporates is one of husband and wife, so that the medium's status is instantly enhanced by marriage to a deity. When the medium channels the god she becomes that god, and as so her statements while in trance are imbued with an authority that is unattainable by any normal mortal man or woman. As a spokesperson for the gods, therefore, the medium's social status is vastly improved thus allowing greater freedoms and increased respect from the community. This does not sound very much like an illness. Indeed, illnesses are never desirable, so it does not make sense to think of spirit possession as a disorder in the context of Ga society, amongst others.[96]

This leads us nicely into a discussion of social-functional theories of spirit possession. As we have already seen in Chapter One, social-functional approaches basically hold that supernatural and religious beliefs, and their associated practices, exist because they perform essential functions within a given society, usually for the purpose of binding society together. As they relate to spirit possession practices, social-functional approaches have generally tended to focus on their ability either to improve social status, as amongst the Ga, or to provide a means for socially repressed individuals to protest against their situation in an acceptable and legitimate manner. The main proponent of this theory has been the social anthropologist I.M. Lewis (1930-2014), whose theory of 'peripheral spirit possession' holds that spirit possession practices enable women to protest against the dominant sex through the incorporation of spirits that essentially take the blame for the woman's actions and utterances while she is possessed. Lewis has characterised such spirit possession practices as little more than 'thinly disguised protest movements directed against the dominant sex.'[97]

More recent theorists, such as cognitive anthropologist Emma Cohen, have suggested that spirit possession practices and experiences can be explained with reference to underlying cognitive processes that are common to all human beings, hence explaining the wide cross-cultural distribution of spirit possession beliefs and practices. Cohen discerns two primary forms of spirit possession: *pathogenic possession*, in which possession by spiritual beings is understood as the underlying cause of illness, and *executive possession*, being the deliberate, and desired, incorporation of spirits, as in mediumship. Cohen suggests that the cognitive processes underlying pathogenic possession are the same as those normally involved in the 'representation of contamination,' while the cognitive faculties involved in executive possession usually deal with 'the world of intentional agents.'[98] From this perspective, then, spirit possession is nothing more than the misinterpretation of otherwise normal cognitive processes - mistakenly attributing spiritual beings to cognitive processes.

The Danger of Oversimplification

There is a tendency towards reductionism in the development of theories of shamanism and spirit possession (as well as in much of Western science more generally), and this often leads to a narrow oversimplification of phenomena that are both multifaceted and complex. Reduction of spirit possession to a mechanism for social protest, for example, ultimately requires that we ignore many other significant factors, chief amongst which are the subjective experiences and beliefs of the possessed themselves. Janice Boddy, an anthropologist who has conducted extensive research into the Zar spirit possession cult of Northern Sudan, has highlighted the importance of considering these mores subtle aspects of the possession experience if we are to gain a real understanding of the phenomenon. She advises that, in order to 'comprehend the scope of possession phenomena, to situate them in their cultural contexts, ethnographers must attend to their informants' experiences of possession and not seek merely to explain them away as something at once less dramatic and more clinical than they appear.'[99] The same might also be said of the cognitive theorists, their abstracted models ultimately become distanced from the lived, experienced, ethnographic reality.[100] To remove spirit possession, or indeed any supernatural practice or experience, from its cultural context and interpret it in alien terms is to lose sight of the true nature of the experience, and what it means to those who undergo it. We will explore the implications of taking the experiences of ethnographic informants seriously in Chapters Six and Seven.

CHAPTER 4

MAGIC & WITCHCRAFT

~

T he modern word 'magic' has its origins in the supposed practices of a mysterious people known as the Magi (who may be recalled from the New Testament book of Matthew following a star in the story of the Nativity). The Magi were, in fact, followers of the Zoroastrian religion, who were famed for their knowledge of astrology, divination and the interpretation of dreams.[101] In the middle ages the term developed a much wider application, being used to refer to all manner of esoteric practices, including the conjuration of spirits. Anthropologists have long been interested in magic: in trying to understand what, from the perspective of modern orthodox Euro-American science, appears to be an utterly irrational form of human thought.[102] Broadly defined, the term magic refers to the belief that human beings can influence and control the physical world through the use of rituals including the manipulation of objects, performance of incantations, giving of offerings, and creation of charms and spells.

Magical Thinking and Superstitions

Magical thinking is becoming an increasingly popular subject for both anthropologists and psychologists interested in understanding magical beliefs and superstitions, and is broadly 'characterised by an absence of differentiation between the self and the natural and social worlds, such that coincidences and correlations are thought to have a causal relationship.[103] Let us take, as an illustrative example, the popular superstition of crossing the fingers for luck. The act and intention of crossing the fingers is believed to have a causal effect in bringing about good fortune, or warding off bad luck. The same might also be said of other superstitions, such as touching wood, throwing salt over the shoulder, or tipping your hat to magpies. It is suggested, therefore, that these characteristic ways of thinking about causal relationships (between internal states and external reality, intentions and events, connections between objects, and so on) are fundamental to the development of superstitious beliefs as well as more advanced systems of magical practice. Magical thinking forms the bedrock for the beliefs and practices we will discuss in this chapter.

Uses of Magic

The ends towards which magic may be used to bring about change in the world fall generally into two broad camps: good, sometimes colloquially referred to as 'white magic,' and its opposite - bad, or 'black' magic. White magic generally involves the performance of rituals, creation of charms and spells for the benefit of the social group, including fertility rituals to ensure bountiful harvests, hunting magic to ensure fruitful hunting expeditions, rituals for healing the sick, ceremonies for extracting evil spirits, and for protecting the community from the attacks of rival magicians.[104] In this respect, then, magic can clearly be thought of as performing an important social function. It is also clear from this brief exposition that the way in which magic is perceived (either as good or bad), is dependent upon the perspective of those involved. A magical attack on a rival group might well be considered 'good' from the perspective of those initiating the attack, and would no doubt be considered 'bad' by those on the receiving end. As with all such concepts, and as we saw in the case of the distinction between shamanism and spirit possession discussed above, it is easy enough to develop analytical categories from the comfort of the library, but when it comes to lived experience in the field, things are not quite so simple.

Divination

Many of the world's cultures employ one or more forms of divination. There are a great may definitions of divination, each with its own particular emphasis, but for the purposes of this chapter a basic definition from *The Oxford English Dictionary* will be sufficient: 'the use of supernatural means to find out about the future or the unknown.' There are many different forms of divinatory practice, and these often form a part of the wider 'magical' world-view of a particular culture. Perhaps the most widely known divinatory practices in the Western world are astrology, which suggests that there are links between astronomical bodies and the world of human life,[105] the Tarot cards, a set of seventy-eight playing cards featuring symbols for interpretation in relation to future life decisions, and coin flipping, with heads for 'yes' and tails for 'no.' Divinatory practices often rely on the interpretation of random processes, or natural phenomena, to assist in decision making - the flipping of a coin represents a random process, the outcome of which must be interpreted by the diviner. In a 1982 lecture on the divinatory practices of the Talensi in Northern Ghana, anthropologist Meyer Fortes (1906-1983) described divination as a process of 'external authorisation of decisions,' and suggested that divination serves the function of both guiding decision making and removing responsibility from the individual.[106]

In his book *Witchcraft, Oracles and Magic among the Azande*, British anthropologist E.E. Evans-Pritchard describes the time he spent living amongst the Azande, a Sudanese farming people, in the 1920s studying their ways of life and belief systems on behalf of the colonial government. The Azande worldview is dominated by notions of witchcraft and divination, which are matters of significant everyday concern (we will return to Azande ideas about witchcraft shortly). Most decisions in the Azande world are made after consulting oracles, of which the Azande have many varieties, the three most popular being:

1. *Dakpa* (the termites oracle)
2. *Iwa* (the rubbing board oracle)
3. *Benge* (the poison oracle)

Benge, or the poison oracle, is the most highly regarded of the Azande's divinatory techniques. Benge involves administering a poisonous red paste to chickens, which causes the chickens to spasm violently, or, on occasion, to die completely. It is from the behaviours of the chicken, while under the influence of the poison, and especially with regard to whether the chicken dies or not, that the Azande 'receive answers to the questions they place before the oracle.' The poison oracle is held in such high regard that its decisions can carry the force of the law. Evans-Pritchard describes how the Azande would consult the poison oracle on any questions that require a serious consideration of evidence. Similarly, all important ventures require authorisation and confirmation from the poison oracle before they are embarked upon.

The Azande would also consult other oracles on matters of everyday importance: the 'rubbing board oracle' (whereby the lid of a rubbing board is rubbed backwards and forwards on the board, with the ease of the rubbing motion being the means by which the oracle's decision is made, that is whether the lid moves smoothly or gets stuck), and the 'termites oracle' (whereby branches from two different trees, *dakpa* and *kpoyo*, are inserted into a termite mound overnight, with the oracle's result determined by which branch has been eaten by the morning). Evans-Pritchard describes how Azande divination is not simply geared towards understanding what is going to happen in the future, or what specific actions to take, rather the 'main purpose of the oracle lies in its ability to reveal the play of mystical forces,' the oracles are, therefore, part of a much wider cosmological scheme, intimately wed, as we will see, with notions of witchcraft.[107]

There are also other forms of divinatory practice that employ altered states of consciousness, especially in the form of spirit possession. Tibetan Buddhism holds its spirit possession oracles in high regard, for example. The Nechung Oracle is the Official State Oracle of Tibet, and lives with the Dalai Lama. The Nechung Oracle may be consulted on governmental issues to provide information and advice in matters of state. The Kuten (medium) is possessed by the Oracle as part of an elaborate ritual during which he adorns brightly coloured clothes, ritual mirrors, and an extremely heavy headdress, requiring support as his trance deepens.[108] In a similar way, anthropologist Nils Bubandt describes how ancestor spirits - usually former Imams and Sultans - are consulted on matters of politics on the island of Ternate in Indonesia, as their disembodied perspectives are greatly respected.[109]

Magical Practitioners

There are many varieties of professional practitioners of magic described in the anthropological literature, but the labels ascribed to each can be vague, confusing and very often overlap with one another. Examples of such terms include shamans, witches, sorcerers, cunning folk, diviners, mediums and medicine-men, amongst others. In an effort to make sense of this confusing array of descriptive terms, in particular those relating to healers of various kinds, anthropologist Michael Winkelman has proposed a typology of what he terms magico-religious practitioners based on the type and scale of society in which they practice, and the specific techniques they employ.[110] See the table below for a summary of Winkelman's main findings, which are based on an in-depth examination of 47 accurately described cultures from the Standard Cross-Cultural Sample database:

Practitioner	Society Type	Techniques & Function
Shaman	Hunter/Gatherer	Use of altered states of consciousness to control spirits and perform a divinatory function.
Shaman/Healer	Hunter/Gatherer	Use of Altered states of consciousness to form relationships with spirit helpers in order to heal the sick, as well as divination.
Healer	Agricultural	Does not necessarily employ altered states of consciousness. Works through rituals, spells and incantations.

Practitioner	Society Type	Techniques & Function
Priest	Agricultural	Does not employ altered states of consciousness. They perform rituals, worship and propitiate gods.
Mediums	Agricultural	Use of altered states of consciousness, in particular trance, to embody spirits. They perform the roles of healer, diviner and propitiator.

Other magico-religious practitioners can be distinguished according to the particular techniques they employ. Sorcerers, for example, can be defined as practitioners of magic employing rituals, incantations and magical objects to intentionally bring about effects in the physical world. Sorcerers, as we shall see, can be differentiated from witches in many African cultural contexts on the grounds that the sorcerer is a *conscious agent* - deliberately seeking to bring about change in the world - while the witch is often thought to be *unconscious* of their magical, and usually malicious, activities.

Experiencing Songhay Sorcery

Between 1976 and 1984, anthropologist Paul Stoller became a sorcerer's apprentice amongst the Songhay people in the Republic of Niger, as part of his ethnographic research. Under the tutelage of the Sorko Benya (sorcerer) Adamu Jenitongo, Stoller 'memorized magical incantantions, ate the special foods of initiation, and participated indirectly in an attack of sorcery that resulted in the temporary facial paralysis of the sister of the intended victim.' The deeper Stoller immersed himself in the world of Songhay sorcery, the more he began to fear the magical attacks of rival sorcerers, until, in 1979, he was forced to return home to America, fearful for his life, after a terrifying attack by a powerful sorcerer:

Suddenly I had the strong impression that something had entered the house. I felt its presence and I was frightened. Set to abandon the house to whatever hovered in the darkness, I started to roll off my mat. But my lower body did not budge...My heart raced. I couldn't flee. What could I do to save myself? Like a sorko benya, I began to recite the genji how, for Adamu Jenitongo had told me that if I ever felt danger I should recite this incantation until I had conquered my fear...I began to feel a slight tingling in my hips...The presence had left the room.[111]

Stoller's encounter with sorcery in the field revealed the powerful nature of magical beliefs and practices as lived experience. He was exposed, first hand, to the dual nature of magic, as simultaneously fascinating and terrifying (recalling Rudolf Otto's dissection of the numinous experience into the *mysterium fascinans* and *mysterium tremedum*). Stoller's experience led him to question the responsibility of the ethnographer working in the field, forcing him to ask whether it was really ethical for an anthropologist to learn the techniques of the sorcerer, or to participate in magical attacks as he had done. His experiences also brought into question the fundamentals of the ethnographic method of participant observation, and in particular the extent to which an ethnographer engaged in such practices can maintain a sense of objective detachment from their research subjects. These are important issues, and we will examine them in greater detail in Chapter Seven.

Theories of Magic

Anthropologists in the nineteenth century, and many still today, considered magic to be a 'primitive' mode of thought. Tylor, referred to it as 'mistaken science,'[112] and Sir James Frazer situated magic in an evolutionary scheme (adapting concepts from Darwinian evolutionary theory to apply to social and cultural change), as the earliest stage in the development of modern science, along a continuum of Magic, Religion and Science. Frazer imagined that primitive humans, in an effort to control their environment, first developed systems of magical belief that provided causal explanations for natural occurrences by, for example, positing the existence of intelligent spirits and connecting principles that controlled nature and could be bargained with or manipulated by magics-religious practitioners. The next stage in Frazer's scheme was the shift from a magical worldview to a religious worldview, in which the spirits, that could once be bargained with, are transformed into more distant deities who may be pleaded with and worshipped, but who were ultimately in control (Frazer reasoned that this shift developed as a result of humanity's inability to influence or change the forces of nature). The final stage, leading to the emergence of science and the scientific method, sees human beings discovering that nature is not governed by intelligent spirits or gods, and that it cannot be bargained or pleaded with. Rather, from this new perspective nature is found to adhere to immutable natural laws. Science then takes its place as the dominant epistemological perspective allowing the discovery of these laws and their manipulation in the form of technology.[113]

While Frazer's evolutionist view may seem to make logical sense, his general approach to anthropology is widely regarded as old-fashioned. His method primarily involved the collection of disparate pieces of information about cultures past and present, from a wide variety of often dubious sources, and then compiling it all to fit his own particular typology. This kind of approach can lead to misrepresentation of the cultures under study. Ethnographers such as E.E. Evans-Pritchard, for example, who conducted actual field-based research, demonstrated that magical beliefs do not preclude rationality, indeed magical beliefs and rationality can, and often do, coincide with one another and so should not necessarily be thought of as any less advanced than scientific notions. In his work amongst the Kiriwina islanders in Papua New Guinea, Bronislaw Malinowski also describes how magical ritual serves as a supplement to practical knowledge, writing that 'without its power and guidance, early man could not have mastered his practical difficulties as he has done.'

In spite of his outdated evolutionary scheme, however, some of Frazer's theories still bare relevance to our attempts at understanding magic. In his epic series of books *The Golden Bough*, for example, Frazer developed a simple classification of two core concepts in many magical traditions: *The Law of Similarity*, and *The Law of Contagion*. The Law of Similarity can be summed up by the phrase 'like produces like.' In other words, magical actions that look like the desired outcome will produce real effects in the real world. A good example of this is in hunting magic, where the act of successfully stalking and killing prey is ritually performed in imitation before the actual hunting expedition to ensure success. The Law of Contagion basically holds that things that have come into contact with each other remain connected, even over great distances. To illustrate this idea, imagine that a magician wants to cause harm to someone. In order to achieve his goal from a distance the magician must get his enemy to touch a particular stone. Once that stone has been touched it is forever linked to the one who touched it. Magical actions can then be carried out on the stone, which will in turn effect the one who touched it. Together, these two laws constitute 'Sympathetic Magic,' which Frazer considered to be the foundation of all magical systems.

Marcel Mauss (1872-1950), the nephew of Émile Durkheim, suggested that magic represented 'the earliest form of human thought,' and that at one time in the distant past humans would only have thought in magical terms. But what would this kind of magical thinking entail? Mauss defined this mode of magical thought as one in which human beings assume that they are 'masters of the external world' in much the same way as they are masters of their own movements. Magic itself, therefore, partakes of this wider way of conceiving of the relationship between consciousness and the physical world - mind over matter. Magic, then, involves the practical application of this more general world-view.

Mauss identified three major components to magic: 1) The Magician (who performs the magic); 2) Magical Representation (the belief in magic); 3) Magical Rites (the actual performed actions). Magical rites are usually performed in private, unlike religious rituals which are usually public events, but they are also dependent upon a wider social belief for their efficacy. For Mauss, then, as for his uncle Durkheim, magic was an essentially social phenomenon, akin to other social institutions such as the legal and religious systems. The major difference between magical and religious rituals, however, is magic's practical application, usually being directed to worldly goals, rather than to metaphysical ends (as religion usually is). It is this practical application that led Mauss to draw comparisons between magic and technology:

> Magic is essentially the art of doing things, and magicians have always taken advantage of their know-how, their dexterity, their manual skill. Magic is the domain of pure production, *ex nihilo*. With words and gestures it does what techniques achieve by labour.[114]

The sociologist Max Weber (1864-1920) charted the decline of magic and religion through a process of what he called disenchantment. He noted the process throughout modern European history, beginning with the rise of Protestantism in the sixteenth century and the Scientific Enlightenment in the seventeenth and eighteenth centuries. Just as Protestantism removed 'superstitious' Roman Catholic ritual from its practices, so rationalist science, and the rise of the Capitalist economic philosophy, rooted out and banished magical ways of thinking and behaving in favour of more 'productive' (in an economic sense), ways of life.[115] Like Frazer, then, Weber saw a very clear progression in which magic and religion are gradually replaced by science and technology. The story, however, is not nearly as simple as this. Indeed, as we have already seen (and will see in our discussion of Witchcraft), magical beliefs and practices continue to persist even within mainstream Euro-American society. Sociologist Peter Berger (1929-2017), for example, writes of the re-enchantment of Western society in his classic sociological study *A Rumour of Angels*:

> For whatever reasons, sizeable numbers of the specimen 'modern man' have not lost a propensity for awe, for the uncanny, for all those possibilities that are legislated against by the canons of secularized rationality. These subterranean rumblings of supernaturalism can, it seems, coexist with all sorts of upstairs rationalism.[116]

More recent scholars have built on the work of Berger, arguing that Weber's disenchantment hypothesis is not entirely accurate. Religious Studies scholar Christopher Partridge, for example, has explored how strands of magical thinking and wider occult beliefs and practices have proliferated in popular culture, and continue to do so - Partridge refers to this undercurrent of Western culture as 'occulture.'[117] Rather than disappearing, then, magical beliefs and practices are transforming - adapting to changes in society as we head deeper into the twenty-first century.

Witchcraft

As with the other topics we have discussed in the preceding chapters, there are many popular assumptions and stereotypes surrounding the subject of witchcraft in modern Western culture. Probably some of the most common images are the three witches from Macbeth, gathered around a boiling cauldron on a windswept hillside prophesying the deaths of kings, and the green-skinned Wicked Witch of the West from L. Frank Baum's *The Wizard of Oz*. Such images are, of course, the product of fantasy (albeit referencing certain features of traditional European folklore). Our modern word 'witch' has its origins in the Old English word *wicce*, which was traditionally used to refer to a female sorceress, or practitioner of magic.[118] Today, a standard dictionary definition of 'witchcraft' reads: 'the practice of magic, especially the use of spells and the calling up of evil spirits.' As we shall see, however, such definitions of witchcraft do not easily apply to practices and beliefs labeled as witchcraft in Non-European societies.

Types of Witchcraft

It is important, therefore, to remember that the use of the term witchcraft is only a very rough translation of the various systems of belief described by anthropologists. As we will see, many of the belief systems and practices that have been labeled 'witchcraft' are very different to what we might come to expect based on popular ideas about what witches are, and what they do. Anthropologist Fiona Bowie has described at least four different ways in which the terms 'witchcraft' and 'witch' are used.

The first usage is in reference to medieval and early modern notions of witchcraft and magic, where magical practices were often split into two distinct categories: good and bad magic. In early modern European parlance good magic was often termed beneficent magic (such as healing the sick, discovering lost objects, and so on), while the phrase maleficent magic, or *maleficium*, was used to refer to deliberate magical rites performed with the intention to cause harm to innocent victims. The widespread belief in *maleficium* was one of the main contributors to the witch-crazes of Europe's early modern period. Secondly, the term witchcraft is often used to refer to perceived Satanic, or overtly anti-Christian, practices. Such images of witchcraft likely emerged as forms of propaganda in the early modern period as a means to discredit pagan beliefs and practices and to further the propagation of the Christian religion. The third usage of the term is in denoting African, as well as other traditional non-European, beliefs and practices: in particular beliefs concerning the causes of misfortune (see the discussion on Azande witchcraft below). And finally, the term has come to be associated with modern Western pagan traditions, such as Wicca, which emerged as significant movements in the twentieth century, and which generally bear little, if any, semblance to either traditional non-European notions of witchcraft, or medieval *maleficium*.[119]

The Witches' Sabbath

During the European witch-hunts of the fourteenth and fifteenth centuries, a period during which people who were believed to be witches were sought out and often executed, it was thought that the souls of witches flew out during sleep to meet for the Witches' Sabbath. The Witches' Sabbath was typically thought to take place in isolated, difficult to reach, locations: on top of mountains or deep in the heart of dense woodland areas. In these places witches were believed to gather in order to participate in mysterious, often blasphemous, rituals. Many researchers have suggested that the medieval belief in the Witches' Sabbath had its origins in pre-Christian pagan practices, often referred to as 'the night ride' or the 'wild hunt.' Popular folk beliefs suggested that witches flew to their sabbath by means of a magical flying ointment, and indeed certain so-called confessions from seventeenth century witches do appear to confirm this idea. As an example, in 1664 an English witch by the name of Elisabeth Style is said to have confessed that before attending the Witches' Sabbath witches would 'anoint their Fore-heads and Hand-Wrists with an Oil the Spirit brings them, which smells raw, and then they are carried in a very short time.' Another witch, by the name of Anne Bishop, from the same county of Somerset, also described how her forehead was 'anointed with a Feather dipt in Oyl' and that soon after 'she hath suddenly been carried to the place of their meeting.'[120] Historian Emma Wilby has suggested that the night-flights of medieval witches may have been remnants of an earlier European shamanic tradition, due particularly to similarities between the shaman's soul-flight to the spirit world and the magical flight of the witch.[121]

Zande Witchcraft

The Azande believe that witchcraft is a physical substance located within the witch's belly, which was believed to be passed down from generation to generation. This substance, known as *mbisimo mangu*, was believed to travel from the body of the witch at night to consume the *mbisimo pasio* - the spiritual essence of the bodily organs of innocent victims. Such attacks, however, were not carried out deliberately by the witch, indeed according to the Azande a witch may not necessarily be aware that they are a witch. Those accused on witchcraft were were often thought to be sleeping when their *mbisimo mangu* went out on its malicious nighttime errands.

Witchcraft was often invoked as an explanation for events in times of misfortune. Instances of misfortune were not understood as the direct result of witchcraft, however, rather witchcraft represented the connecting principle that linked a particular chain of events. Evans-Pritchard provides a particularly illuminating example of this connecting principle in his description of a granary collapse in a Zande village:

> In Zandeland sometimes an old granary collapses. There is nothing remarkable in this. Every Zande knows that termites eat the supports in course of time and that even the hardest woods decay after years of service. Now a granary is the summerhouse of a Zande homestead and people sit beneath it in the heat of the day and chat or play... Consequently it may happen that there are people beneath the granary when it collapses and they are injured...Now why should these particular people have been sitting under this particular granary at the particular moment when it collapsed?...The Zande knows that the supports were undermined by termites and that people were sitting beneath the granary in order to escape the heat and glare of the sun. But he knows besides why these two events occurred at a precisely similar moment in time and space. It was due to the action of witchcraft. If there had been no witchcraft people would not have been sitting under the granary and it would not have fallen on them, or it would have collapsed but the people would not have been sheltering under it at the time. Witchcraft explains the coincidence of these two happenings.

Witchcraft (known as *mangu*) was therefore conceived as an unconscious force and so was contrasted with sorcery (*gbegere ngua*), which was understood to be a deliberate, usually malicious, performance of ritual magical acts. A sorcerer, then, was in control of their malicious actions, while a witch was not.[122]

Witches and Unwitchers in Rural France and the Evil Eye

In the 1970s the French anthropologist Jeanne Favret-Saada conducted fieldwork in an area of rural France known as the Bocage. Favret-Saada found a strong current of belief in witchcraft in the region, persisting even in the latter half of the twentieth century. The witchcraft beliefs of the rural communities she investigated, much as those of the Azande, were intimately entwined with notions of misfortune, especially in the case of an unlikely string of misfortunate events. A single unfortunate occurrence, for example the death of some livestock, would not necessarily be interpreted as the result of witchcraft, but if this event occurred coincidentally alongside other misfortunes, such as family illness, a car crash, and a bad crop yield, then a deliberate act of witchcraft begins to appear more likely. Again, witchcraft is the connecting principle. Once an individual suspects that they are the victim of witchcraft, they will seek out the assistance of an 'unwitcher,' a professional magician, to perform specific rites to counter the malicious attacks of the supposed witch, who may be a jealous neighbour, or any other member of the local community.[123]

Closely related to this notion of misfortune stemming from the jealously of a neighbour is the widespread complex of beliefs often referred to as 'The Evil Eye.' Simply defined, Evil Eye beliefs hold that harm (illness in the case of living things, or damage in the case of inanimate objects), may be caused simply by the jealous gaze of another individual. In order to combat such misfortune many cultures use special apotropaic (evil deflecting) charms, gestures and formulae that serve to reflect the Evil Eye back onto the jealous individual.[124] A common, highly visible, example of an apotropaic charm for countering the Evil Eye is the small blue and white glass eye charm that can often be seen hanging in homes and shops in Turkey, Greece and other Mediterranean countries.

Wicca and Other Neo-Paganisms

As we saw in relation to Neo-Shamanism in the previous chapter, there was a proliferation of movements in the twentieth century that sought to reconnect with traditional systems of magical belief. Arguably the most famous of such movements is Wicca. First codified as a distinct movement by retired civil servant and amateur anthropologist

Gerald Gardner (1886–1964), Wicca combined many different facets of traditional pagan beliefs with aspects of Freemasonry and Aleister Crowley's (1875-1947) Thelemic tradition of Ceremonial Magic. In the 1930s, while also a member of the Esoteric Rosicrucian Order, Gardner claimed to have discovered a secret Coven practicing witchcraft in the New Forest, and considered them to be a survival of much more ancient practices - a theory that he borrowed from the controversial Egyptologist Margaret Murray (1863-1963).[125] Murray believed that she had discovered, through her historical researches, an unbroken line of pagan practice going right back into prehistory, that continued to flourish in secret despite centuries of religious persecution. She wrote of secret covens of thirteen individuals who would gather to worship a horned god, who, she argued, had been transformed into the popular image of the devil by anti-pagan propagandists. Much of Murray's work on the witchcraft cult has been criticised on the grounds of her selective scholarship, choosing only those sources that seemed to fit her thesis, but the influence of her books on the development of Neo-Pagan religions was undoubtedly a significant one.

As with Neo-Shamanisms, like Michael Harner's core shamanism, Neo-Pagan movements have had their authenticity questioned, primarily on the basis of their reinterpretation and adaptation of traditional beliefs. This kind of mixing of ideas is referred to as syncretism, and is by no means a hallmark of new religious movements alone, indeed even major world religions syncretically incorporate elements of traditional, as well as other major, religions. The question of authenticity is, therefore, a strange one as no cultural system is immune from the influences of others.

General Theories of Witchcraft

The majority of theories of witchcraft are functionalist in nature, usually explaining witchcraft beliefs as social mechanisms for explaining misfortune, combatting potential socially destructive issues, such as interpersonal jealousy, and releasing social tensions. Such theories often refer to witches as scapegoats onto whom negative social tensions are projected. Evans-Pritchard's approach to Azande witchcraft, and Favret-Saada's approach to witchcraft in the Bocage, might be defined as intellectualist, in that they treat witchcraft as a model for explaining misfortune, in particular a series of misfortunate events that would otherwise be difficult to explain. Pamela J. Stewart and Andrew Strathern have argued that intellectualist and functionalist accounts of witchcraft both provide useful insights, but that both need to be brought together in order to develop a more complete understanding of the phenomenon. They suggested that witchcraft can be understood in relation to other social phenomena such as gossip and rumour. Accusations of witchcraft usually occur in small communities, where 'rumour and gossip tend to feed on and contribute to patterns of uncertainty in human communication that are intertwined with the probability of misunderstanding and conflict.'[126] Misunderstandings and conflict may, then, lead to accusations of witchcraft. Such theories, while they do apply to traditional African and European witchcraft beliefs, do not necessarily relate to the development of modern Neo-Pagan witchcraft traditions. These might best be understood from the perspective of changing trends in religiosity and spirituality, and as an effort to reconnect with traditional ways of thought.

Of course, none of these approaches takes seriously the possibility that there might also be genuine paranormal experiences, of one form or another, involved. It is for this reason that the immersive fieldwork of ethnographers like Jeanne Favret-Saada and Paul Stoller are so important, because they fill in the experiential gaps in our theory making that are left over after sociological and intellectualist approaches have been applied. They show that, above and beyond the sociological and intellectualist functions of witchcraft and sorcery there is an experiential, lived, reality to such systems of practice and belief that simply cannot be ignored.

CHAPTER 5

ETHNOGRAPHY AND THE PARANORMAL

~

Immersing yourself in another culture is always going to be a strange experience, and most anthropologists will be expecting to encounter different ways of thinking about the world when they first embark on their fieldwork. What they do not necessarily expect, however, is to start *experiencing* the world around them differently - to begin seeing and feeling things that, from the perspective of western science, simply cannot be possible. We might class such experiences, therefore, as 'anomalous' because they do not sit comfortably with the rationalist world-view of scientific materialism, but that is not to say that such experiences are considered anomalous by the ethnographer's host culture. As we have seen in the previous chapters of this book, while such experiences may not be particularly common or widespread amongst the population of the host culture, they may yet have a place - and significant meaning - in that culture's broader world-view. In other cultures around the world experiences such as telepathic communication between two individuals, predicting the future in dreams, seeing the dead re-animate, witnessing apparitions, communicating with spirits through entranced mediums, or being afflicted by witchcraft may be entirely possible.

Many highly respected academic anthropologists, in conducting ethnographic fieldwork amongst other cultures, have gone several steps beyond appreciating different modes of thinking about the world and have crossed the threshold into alternate ways of experiencing it.

E.B. Tylor, E.E. Evans-Pritchard, Bruce T. Grindal and Edith Turner all crossed this threshold during their fieldwork, and all interpreted and presented their experiences in different ways. Through examining the ways in which these ethnographers documented their experiences, and how their personal world-views transformed to accommodate such unusual phenomena, it is possible to gain an insight into both changing academic attitudes towards the anomalous and the mysterious nature of the paranormal itself.

Raps, Trances and Victorian Anthropology

As we have already seen, E.B. Tylor is widely regarded as one of the founding figures of anthropology, and is also held up as the epitome of the so-called 'armchair anthropologist.' In spite of a brief fieldwork trip to Mexico, Tylor preferred to carry out his research in the comfort of his library rather than in the field amongst the people he wrote about. It is a little known fact, however, that Tylor conducted a form of ethnographic fieldwork in London in 1872 with some of the most prominent mediums of the burgeoning Spiritualist movement, which had spread rapidly across America and Europe since its advent in New York State in 1848. Tylor was intrigued, as indeed were many of the Victorian intellectual community, by the radical claims of the Spiritualists to be able to demonstrate the continued existence of human personality after death. Belief in spiritual beings was to become the central theme of Tylor's hugely influential theory for the origin of religion (see Chapter 1), and it has been suggested by the historian of anthropology George Stocking Jr. (1928-2013) that his ideas concerning animism developed in parallel with his researches into the Spiritualist movement.

Tylor saw Spiritualism as a modern remnant, what he termed a 'survival,' of primitive animist beliefs and as such was keen to gain firsthand personal experience of the movement: to essentially observe animism in action. Tylor embarked upon his fieldwork as a sceptic convinced that Spiritualist mediums possessed at best a 'deluded belief' in the efficacy of their performances or, at worst, a malicious desire to con unsuspecting individuals with deliberate acts of fraud. Tylor's personal field-notes from the time, however, reveal a much more ambiguous state of affairs. Indeed, although Tylor did detect evidence of deliberate fraud in the performances of some of the mediums he observed, with others - most notably the famous mediums Daniel

Dunglas Home (1833-1886), the Reverend Stainton Moses (1839-1892) and Kate Fox (1837-1892) - Tylor had some rather unusual experiences that challenged his initial sceptical standpoint. After a séance with Home, for example, Tylor wrote in his private diary that he had 'failed to make out how either raps, table-levitation, or accordion-playing were produced.' With Stainton Moses he described how '[h]is trance seemed real,' and concluded that his experience with Kate Fox was 'very curious, and her feats are puzzling to me,' noting that her phenomena 'deserve further looking into.' Tylor's experiences with these mediums forced him to admit, in his own words, 'a prima facie case on evidence' for the abilities of certain mediums and to state that he could not deny the possibility 'that there may be a psychic force causing raps, movements, levitations, etc.'

Regardless of his experiences with the Spiritualists, and his inability to account for them in any normal terms, Tylor did not see it fit - or even at all necessary - to publish these observations in his public writings on animism. Tylor's experiences, it could be argued, seemed to imply that such experiences were not by any stretch of the imagination limited to the so-called 'primitives,' but could in-fact be had by anyone, including members of the Victorian intelligentsia. In the face of ridicule from the scientific community, as later happened in the case of the pioneering chemist and physicist Sir William Crookes (1832-1919) when he published his findings in support of D.D. Home's mediumship in 1874, Tylor opted to keep his anomalous experiences to himself.[127]

Anomalous Lights among the Azande

By the beginning of the twentieth century anthropological methods had made several major advances since Tylor's day. Armchair anthropology of the Tylor and Frazer variety was out of fashion, and good ethnographic research, following the methodological developments advocated by Bronislaw Malinowski, required that the ethnographer engage with the society being studied in as intimate a way as possible. This approach to fieldwork came to be called 'participant observation,' and has since become the central pillar of contemporary ethnographic theory and practice. As we have already seen, in 1926 E.E. Evans-Pritchard was employed by the colonial British government to learn more about the beliefs and life-ways of the Azande people in the Sudan. In order to do this Evans-Pritchard lived amongst the Azande, on-and-off, for four consecutive years and participated, to the best of his abilities, in the everyday life of the village he lived in. Through this process of intimate interaction with the Azande people Evans-Pritchard came to an appreciation of fundamental differences in the cosmological and metaphysical systems of the colonial British and the Azande, particularly concerning the way in which the Azande attributed causality to occurrences (see discussion in Chapter 4). Furthermore, the anthropologist learned that the Azande world-view was by no means an irrational one. Indeed, Evans-Pritchard concluded, quite radically at the time, that Azande beliefs were in fact logical, and that belief in witchcraft was not incompatible with a rational appreciation of nature. It was within this cultural context, late one night while writing up field-notes in his hut, that Evans-Pritchard had his own anomalous experience. He writes:

> About midnight, before retiring, I took a spear and went for my usual nocturnal stroll. I was walking in the garden at the back of the hut, amongst banana trees, when I noticed a bright light passing at the back of my servant's hut towards the homestead of a man called Tupoi. As this seemed worth investigation I followed its passage until a grass screen obscured the view. I ran quickly through my hut to the other side in order to see where the light was going to, but did not regain sight of it. I knew that only one man, a member of my household, had a lamp that might have given off so bright a light, but next morning he told me that he had neither been out late at night nor had he used his lamp. There did not lack ready informants to tell me that what I had seen was witchcraft. Shortly afterwards, on the same morning, an old relative of Tupoi and an inmate of his household died. This fully explained the light I had seen. I never discovered the real origin, which was probably a handful of grass lit by someone on his way to defecate, but the coincidence of the direction along which the light moved and the subsequent death accorded well with Zande ideas.

To the Azande, then, the phenomenon witnessed by the anthropologist that night was clearly of supernatural origin - it was witchcraft-substance (*mbisimo mangu*), a mysterious substance believed to reside inside the body of witches, unconsciously externalized and sent out on murderous errands. However, despite the conviction of his informants that what he had seen was disembodied witchcraft, Evans-Pritchard suggests that it was 'probably a handful of grass lit by someone on his way to defecate.' This explaining away of the experience entirely ignored the Azande interpretation of the phenomenon, though Evans-Pritchard was clearly aware of the significance of such experiences within the Zande world-view.[128]

It is interesting to note at this point that in 1944 Evans-Pritchard became a convert to Roman Catholicism, and it has been suggested that his fieldwork experiences with African religious systems motivated this dramatic shift in perspective. It could be argued, therefore, that Evans-Pritchard's conversion to the Catholic faith was a means to reconcile his personal world-view with his experiences in the field. Such a transformation, combined with a willingness to publish his experience publicly (despite explaining it away), represents a distinct departure from E.B. Tylor's complete suppression of his own anomalous fieldwork experiences seventy years earlier.

The Dancing Dead in Sisala Death Divination

American anthropologist Bruce T. Grindal's anomalous experience - or in his own terms 'altered, or supernatural' experience - occurred amongst the Sisala people of Ghana in October 1967. Following the ominously close deaths of two members of the same village it was deduced that the resultant funeral would be a 'hot' event 'involving ritual danger, or *bomo*.' Grindal's ethnographic account of this incident included several days leading up to the funeral in which the author's daily routine was significantly disrupted, so that by the time of the funeral, and the 'death divination' that accompanied it, he was physically and mentally exhausted. His description of the event is so rich in detail that it seems only fair to present it in its entirety, rather than attempt to summarize the experience and reduce its complexity:

> As I watched them I became intensely aware of their back-and-forth motion. I began to see the goka and the corpse tied together in the undulating rhythms of the singing, the beating of the iron hoes, and the movement of feet and bodies. Then I saw the corpse jolt and occasionally pulsate, in a counterpoint to the motions of the goka. At first I thought that my mind was playing tricks with my eyes, so I cannot say when the experience first occurred; but it began with moments of anticipation and terror, as though I knew something unthinkable was about to happen. The anticipation left me breathless, gasping for air. In

the pit of my stomach I felt a jolting and tightening sensation, which corresponded to moments of heightened visual awareness. What I saw in those moments was outside the realm of normal perception. From both the corpse and goka came flashes of light so fleeting that I cannot say exactly where they originated. The hand of the goka would beat down the iron hoe, the spit would fly from his mouth, and suddenly the flashes of light flew like sparks from a fire. Then I felt my body become rigid. My jaws tightened and at the base of my skull I felt a jolt as though my head had been snapped off my spinal column. A terrible and beautiful sight burst upon me. Stretching from the amazingly delicate fingers and mouths of the goka, strands of fibrous light played upon the head, fingers, and toes of the dead man. The corpse, shaken by spasms, then rose to its feet, spinning and dancing in a frenzy. As I watched, convulsions in the pit of my stomach tied not only my eyes but also my whole being into this vortex of power. It seemed that the very floor and walls of the compound had come to life, radiating light and power, drawing the dancers in one direction and then another. Then a most wonderful thing happened. The talking drums on the roof of the dead man's house began to glow with a light so strong that it drew the dancers to the rooftop. The corpse picked up the drumsticks and began to play.

Such an intense experience as this could hardly have been ignored, and Grindal's determination to document and publish it in such vivid detail, and in accordance with the Sisala's own interpretation of the events, is evidential of a shift in anthropological acceptance of anomalous occurrences and indigenous interpretations of them. In concluding his discussion of this unusual experience Grindal confirmed that it definitely happened as described, and that others present at the time saw the same things that he did. Grindal used this experience as a gateway towards understanding Sisala culture. By sharing this experience with the Sisala community he had essentially become one of the people he was studying. Nevertheless, and perhaps unsurprisingly, this experience was too much for Grindal, who noted in his write-up that he was happy to leave it as a once in a lifetime experience. He felt no further compulsion to go in search of similar experiences, preferring to look back on it philosophically from the comfort of his office.[129]

Drawing Out the Ihamba Spirit

Edith Turner's unusual fieldwork experience with the Ndembu in Zambia is perhaps the most widely discussed ethnographic encounter with the paranormal, and has been very influential to the emerging generation of anthropologists of the paranormal. Turner's famous account details her participation in the Ihamba healing ceremony, a long and intense ritual during which the ritual doctor (Singleton) attempted to remove the malignant Ihamba spirit from an afflicted patient (Meru). At the culmination of this particular ceremony Turner saw with her own eyes an unusual plasma-like mass being extracted from the patient's back:

> And just then, through my tears, the central figure swayed deeply: all leaned forward, this was indeed going to be it. I realised along with them that the barriers were breaking - just as I let go in tears. Something that wanted to be born was now going to be born. Then a certain palpable social integument broke and something calved along with me. I felt the spiritual motion, a tangible feeling of breakthrough going through the whole group. Then Meru fell - the spirit event first and the action afterward...Quite an interval of struggle elapsed while I clapped like one possessed, crouching beside Bill amid a lot of urgent talk, while [the witch-doctor] pressed Meru's back, guiding and leading out the tooth - Meru's face in a grin of tranced passion, her back quivering rapidly. Suddenly Meru raised her arm, stretched it in liberation, and I saw with my own eyes a giant thing emerging out of the flesh of her back. This thing was a large gray blob about six inches across, a deep gray opaque thing emerging as a sphere. I was amazed - delighted. I still laugh with glee at the realisation of having seen it, the ihamba, and so big! We were all just one in triumph. The gray thing was actually out there, visible, and you could see Singleton's hands working and scrabbling on the back- and then the thing was there no more. Singleton had it in his pouch, pressing it in with his other hand as well. The receiving can was ready; he transferred whatever it was into the can and capped the castor oil leaf and bark lid over it. It was done.

For Edith Turner this experience was so powerful that it called into question all of the traditional methodologies and theoretical positions of social anthropology. She realised that for decades anthropologists had been completely ignoring the claims of their informants to the existence of spirits. She writes: 'again and again anthropologists witness spirit rituals, and again and again some indigenous exegete tries to explain that spirits are present...and the anthropologist proceeds to interpret them differently.' Turner's solution to this problem was to cast aside the strictures of 'positivists' denial,' as she termed it, and to encourage anthropologists to learn to 'see what the Natives see' in the course of their fieldwork. This approach goes beyond anthropology's traditional position of maintaining an 'objective' distance between the ethnographer and the society under study, and plunges headfirst into a completely new way of interpreting and experiencing the world. Moreover, Turner's personal perspective on spirit beliefs was radically altered by this experience, prompting her to move in the direction of considering spirits as ontologically real entities - a real challenge to the established secular and materialist frameworks of the social sciences.[130]

Towards an Anthropology of the Paranormal

What, if any, conclusions can be drawn from this small collection of anecdotal reports? One of the most significant insights is that anomalous experiences such as these can be had by anyone, especially if they participate fully and immersively in the relevant cultures and ritual situations. This would appear to be a fundamental aspect of the paranormal in general - it requires our participation in the moment to be experienced, whether spontaneously or in a ritualized context. Indeed, it is interesting to note at this juncture the work of the French ethnologist Lucien Lévy-Bruhl (1857-1939) who argued that 'participation' was a fundamental characteristic of what he termed 'primitive mentality.' According to Lévy-Bruhl 'mystical participation' is a mode of engaging with the world that sees connections between internal and external states - a form of magical thinking and experiential engagement fundamental to understanding magic and the supernatural.[131] E.B. Tylor left the comfort of his study to conduct fieldwork in Spiritualist seances and in so doing exposed himself to phenomena for which he could find no rational explanation; Evans-Pritchard was fully immersed in Azande culture and belief when he encountered disembodied witchcraft floating through the air in the African bush; Bruce Grindal's encounter with the *mysterium tremendum* occurred in the midst of a traditional Sisala death divination after several days of disrupted daily routine; and Edith Turner's 'breakthrough moment' erupted when she finally let go of her emotions and fully participated in the Ihamba ceremony.

These illuminating insights into the nature of the paranormal are precisely the reason that ethnographic methodologies should be used to supplement parapsychology's laboratory-based experiments (see Chapters Six and Seven). The ethnographic approach lends itself to a greater appreciation of the wider context in which paranormal experiences and phenomena occur: it demonstrates the role of culture in such events, both in terms of the ways in which such phenomena manifest and the way they are interpreted by those who experience them. The element of participation allows the researcher to experience first-hand the phenomena they are investigating and reveals the significance of alternate states of consciousness and emotional engagement in experiences of the paranormal. These accounts also demonstrate a gradual shift in the way that anthropologists have dealt with anomalous experiences in the field. The move towards a greater reflexivity on behalf of the ethnographer has led to an emphasis on the anthropology of experience, which in turn has prompted certain anthropologists to consider the ontology of the anomalous phenomena they witness in the field. Further ethnographic research in this direction may reveal yet more fascinating insights into the nature and experience of the paranormal, and we will explore what an anthropology of the paranormal might look like in the final chapter of this book.

CHAPTER 6

PSYCHICAL RESEARCH AND
PARAPSYCHOLOGY

~

Now that we have surveyed a sample of the wide variety of supernatural beliefs and practices prevalent throughout the world, we have to ask why such beliefs and practices are so persistent and widespread amongst human beings. As we saw in Chapter One anthropology has generally tended towards two primary interpretations of supernatural beliefs and their associated practices. The first holds that supernatural beliefs are the product of underlying cognitive and psychological processes, or serve psychological functions in providing reassurance against uncontrollable factors. The second dominant interpretation suggests that supernatural belief systems exist to serve sociological functions. Both of these positions ultimately hold that there is no reality underlying supernatural belief systems, other than misperception and the misinterpretation of otherwise 'normal' processes.

A third possibility is that the native interpretation is correct: that when the shaman claims to visit the spirit-world during trance, she really does leave her body to converse with spiritual intelligences; that the spiritual healer really can do what he says he can; that the informant really did see a ghost, and so on. This is a perspective that is very rarely taken seriously by anthropologists. Indeed, it is often argued that an anthropologist who has come to accept the beliefs of their informants has lost their objectivity - they are said to have 'gone native.'

If there is one thing that anthropology has clearly demonstrated, however, it is that there are innumerable different ways of living in and experiencing the world that are equally well-adapted. This poses a challenge to the assumed dominance of the materialist-scientific worldview. How can we be sure that the worldview we have come to accept as dominant is really the best suited for accurately describing the universe? Could it be that worldviews which take seriously the possibility of, for example, non-physical intelligences and mind-to-mind communication, are better suited to understanding the universe than the strongly materialistic worldview of contemporary Western science? To take seriously such questions is to open up a whole new realm of inquiry for anthropology.

This chapter, and the chapter that follows it, will address some of the broader implications of the ideas presented in this book, especially with regard to the nature of paranormal experiences, which seem to be fairly regular occurrences in practically every human culture, past and present. Particular emphasis will be placed on the development of a wider perspective that can enable a scientific, cross-cultural, examination of paranormal experience without the need for the excessive reduction of people's experiences to overly simplified constructs.

In order to do this I will expand our perspective out from a purely anthropological one to examine some of the theories that have developed in the field of parapsychology, a discipline specifically concerned with understanding the human capacity for paranormal experience. This chapter will give a brief historical overview of the development of parapsychology and its key findings, so that in the next chapter we might explore some of the ways in which parapsychological and anthropological approaches can interact and shed new light on supernatural beliefs and paranormal experiences.

The emphasis on parapsychological research in this chapter, then, can be taken in two ways. The first is as validation of certain aspects of the supernatural beliefs discussed in this book, and for many this might be considered a step too far. Another way in which this chapter might be read is as an effort towards what anthropologist Fiona Bowie calls 'cognitive empathetic engagement' with other world-views.[132] Examining the evidence from parapsychology, as it relates to the ethnographic data of anthropology, could be seen as another way of taking the beliefs and experiences of ethnographic informants seriously, and of interpreting them through frames of reference that are neither dismissive nor reductionist.

In a similar vein, we might interpret the parapsychological data from a 'possibilian' perspective - that is a theoretical position designed to overcome the repetition and tedium associated with the contemporary debate between atheism and theism, and proposed by neuroscientist David Eagleman. Eagleman is of the opinion that this intense form of polarisation leads to a false dichotomy - either there is a God, or there is not - whereas, in actuality, there is a great deal more that we could be talking about and exploring in between: the possibilities are endless. Possibilianism emphasises the fact of our ignorance and embraces it, arguing that we simply don't know enough about existence to cling ardently to a single hypothesis. In light of this, then, Eagleman has proposed what he calls a 'possibility space,' within which all possible hypotheses are equal until sufficient evidence is available to either reject or accept one or more hypothesis. A possibilian holds multiple potential hypotheses in mind simultaneously, and is comfortable with this stance. It is intended to be an exploratory and creative position that, to my mind, succeeds where other standpoints have failed in its ability to rationally consider alternative hypotheses without recourse to reductionism and narrow-mindedness.[133] I have more recently developed this idea further into the concept of 'ontological flooding.'[134] Through attempting to interpret supernatural beliefs and experiences from the perspective that there is, at the very least, a possibility that they might be real, and combining this with a parapsychological viewpoint that attempts to understand the different processes involved in the production of anomalous experiences, we can move towards a more empathetic, and perhaps more accurate, understanding of what such experiences mean to those whose world-view is inclusive of the paranormal and the supernatural.

We will begin, therefore, with a brief introduction to parapsychology, a discipline that has been actively engaged in the study of the nature of paranormal phenomena for over 130 years. Anthropologists investigating supernatural beliefs and practices in the field would do well to have at least a partial understanding of some of the findings of this impressive body of research, whether they interpret such findings as evidence in support of traditional supernatural beliefs, or as valuable data for developing a more empathetic perspective. This chapter is not, by any means, an exhaustive overview of the parapsychological literature, as this would require a much larger book than this, but it is hoped that it will provide a useful starting point for further inquiry, for those whose interest is piqued.

The Origins of Parapsychology

Mesmerism

As we have seen in previous chapters, there is evidence to suggest that human beings have been having experiences that we would class as supernatural or paranormal since at least as far back as the Palaeolithic period in the form of shamanic encounters with altered realities. It wasn't until several thousand years later, however, in the eighteenth and nineteenth centuries, that a concerted scientific effort to study these kinds of experiences was undertaken.

The first steps towards a critical science of the supernatural were taken in response to the claims of a German physician by the name of Franz Anton Mesmer (1734-1815), who believed he had discovered a new form of energy present within the human body. Mesmer discovered that he was able to cure the illnesses of his patients simply by staring them in the eyes, pressing his thumbs into theirs, and passing his hands over afflicted parts of the body. These movements induced trances and strong uncontrollable convulsions in his patients - so-called 'magnetic crises' that ultimately produced a cure for their illnesses. He explained these seemingly miraculous effects as resulting from the manipulation of a magnetic fluid that permeates and flows through the human body, and connects us to the wider cosmos. He called this fluid 'animal magnetism.'[135]

The apparent success of Mesmer's cures captured the popular imagination, and before long he had become something of a celebrity, attracting high profile patients from the upper echelons of European society. His success, however, also attracted a great deal of interest from other more traditional physicians of the day, as well as a fair amount of sceptical suspicion. This culminated in 1784 when King Louis XVI of France appointed a commission of leading scientific thinkers, including the famous American scientist and politician Benjamin Franklin (1706-1790), to investigate Mesmer's claims. The commission's report came back stating that Mesmer's cure was purely down to the imagination, and yet, despite this setback, the craze for animal magnetism continued to flourish.

Later, one of Mesmer's students, the Marquis de Puysegur (1751-1825), found that dramatic convulsions where not a requirement of the mesmeric trance, and instead worked to promote what he termed a 'gentle crisis' in which the patient would be induced into a state of trance and then conversed with in order to get to the bottom of their ailments, essentially predicting the development of Freudian psychoanalysis in the late nineteenth century.[136] Another interesting side-effect of this treatment was the discovery that individuals in the mesmeric state seemed to exhibit unusual abilities such as clairvoyance, the ability to diagnose illnesses and, interestingly, a 'community of sensation' between the magnetiser and the magnetised. In other words, they were apparently able to share physical and emotional sensations at a distance (telepathy) during the mesmeric state. While these seemingly supernatural side-effects were shunned by the medical establishment, the therapeutic efficacy of mesmerism was eventually welcomed into the halls of science, albeit under the new title of 'hypnosis' or 'hypnotism,' coined by the Scottish surgeon James Braid (1795-1860) in 1842, who demonstrated the power of hypnotic states by conducting amputations using trances instead of anaesthetics.[137]

The apparent clairvoyant abilities of individuals in the mesmeric state eventually took on a life of their own. Sideshows that blurred the lines between science, medicine and performance toured throughout Europe and America demonstrating the wonders of animal magnetism to the amazement of public audiences, and thus became hugely popular sources of entertainment and intrigue. As the nineteenth century progressed mesmeric demonstrations of clairvoyance and community of sensation became subsumed into the emerging movement known as Modern Spiritualism, which was to take the Euro-American world by storm and would have an important role to play in the development of parapsychology.[138]

Spiritualism

The official birth date of the Spiritualist movement (though there were clear precursors to it throughout history), is generally held to be the 31st of March 1848 when, in the small town of Hydesville in New York State, the home of the Fox family became the locus of some unusual paranormal activity. The Fox family was plagued by perplexing bangs and knocks on the walls and ceiling of their modest wooden house. In an effort to make sense of what was going on the two youngest sisters of the family, Kate and Margaret, began to address the knocks as though they were being produced by an invisible intelligence. The sisters soon realised that they could communicate with this apparently invisible agent through a simple code of knocks, one for 'Yes' and two for 'No.' In this way the sisters learned that the intelligence behind the knocks was the spirit of a pedlar by the name of Charles B. Rosma (though the sisters often referred to the spirit as Mr. Splitfoot), who claimed to have been murdered in the house some years before the Fox family moved in. News of the Fox sisters and their apparent ability to communicate with invisible spirits spread rapidly across the United States and Europe leaving a trail of individuals discovering their own ability to communicate with the dead by a variety of different means: from raps and bangs, through ouija boards, trance and physical mediumship.[139]

Perhaps the most influential innovator in early physical mediumship was the Scottish-born medium Daniel Dunglas Home. After an early life allegedly filled with spiritual visions and premonitions, and coming from a long line of Scottish seers, Home conducted his first séance at the age of eighteen and swiftly gained a reputation as a powerful medium. By 1856 Home was conducting séances in Britain, and in 1868 he performed his most famous paranormal feat: the levitation of his body horizontally out through a third-story window at Ashley House in London. This event was witnessed by Lord Lindsay, Lord Adare and Captain Charles Wynne, all men of high repute and considered at the time to be honest in what they described.[140]

In 1874 Home's mediumship received further support with the publication of a report by the physicist Sir William Crookes. The report presented experimental evidence that Home was indeed able to manipulate physical objects by paranormal means. Using specially designed laboratory equipment Crookes tested Home's ability to change the weight of physical objects and to play tunes on an accordion suspended out of reach in a cage. Home's séances also often featured the alleged materialization of glowing hands that would mischievously touch the sitters.[141]

Arthur Conan Doyle (1859-1930), the world-famous creator of Sherlock Holmes, considered D.D. Home to be something of a spiritual virtuoso. Conan Doyle argued that Home was proficient in four different forms of mediumship: the direct voice (whereby spirits communicate verbally, independent of the medium), trance mediumship (whereby spirits communicate verbally through the body of the medium), clairvoyance (the ability to see visions of the spirit world, the future and distant locations) and physical mediumship (the ability to psychically manipulate physical objects). These would become hallmarks phenomena of Spiritualist seances across America and Europe right until the present day.

The Society for Psychical Research

In 1882 the Society for Psychical Research (SPR) was established. It was established by the Cambridge scholars Henry Sidgwick (1838-1900), Eleanor Sidgwick (1845-1936), F.W.H. Myers (1843-1901) and Edmund Gurney (1847-1888), and was the first organisation devoted to the scientific study of the paranormal. Indeed, the stated aim of the SPR was to investigate 'that large body of debatable phenomena designated by such terms as mesmeric, psychical and spiritualistic in the same spirit of exact and unimpassioned enquiry which has enabled Science to solve so many problems.' This was the birth of psychical research, the scientific study of the paranormal.

The early investigations of the SPR were divided into six separate, though often closely related, committees dealing with:

1) thought transference and mesmerism,
2) Mediumship and survival,
3) odic forces (subtle energies),
4) apparitions and hauntings,
5) physical phenomena and;
6) the history of psychical experiences.

The Society for Psychical Research quickly gained a reputation for serious investigation of claims to the paranormal, in particular the investigation of Spiritualist mediums, many of whom, though by no means all, were declared fraudulent by SPR researchers. One of the Society's earliest (and lasting) contributions was the collection and analysis of hundreds of reports of hallucinations experienced by people from all levels of British society, and published in 1886 as the *Census of Hallucinations*. Amongst these reports SPR researchers identified several so-called 'veridical hallucinations,' defined as hallucinations that seemed to contain information that the experiencer could not possibly have had access to by any normal means. It was the opinion of many members of the Society that such data represented substantial evidence in favour of the existence of telepathy (a term coined by F.W.H. Myers), or the ability to transmit information directly from one mind to another bypassing the usual physical means of communication. Telepathy was to become the bedrock of psychical research, the principle process underlying many paranormal experiences.[142]

From Psychical Research to Parapsychology

For the most part the work of the SPR was focused on the investigation of spontaneous cases - often after they had taken place - and this had a negative impact on the way in which the theories of psychical researchers were perceived by the wider scientific community. By the early years of the twentieth century science had practically become synonymous with the idea of replicability in experimental research, with scientific research in physics, chemistry and biology increasingly conducted in carefully controlled laboratory environments. The same was true for the burgeoning psychological sciences, which followed the model of the psychological laboratory first developed by the German psychologist Wilhelm Wundt (1832-1920) in 1879. In order to bring psychical research up to date with modern laboratory-based methods a young psychologist by the name of Joseph Banks Rhine (1895-1980) - along with one of psychology's early pioneers, Professor William McDougall (1871-1938) - established the first psychical research laboratory at Duke University in 1930. In order to differentiate this new laboratory based research from the field research of the SPR, Rhine and McDougall coined the term 'parapsychology,' borrowed from the German term *parapsychologie*, first used by the psychologist Max Dessoir (1867-1947) in 1889. J.B. Rhine's contribution to parapsychology was immense. The laboratory at Duke University established parapsychology as a scientific, if somewhat controversial, discipline and provided much of the groundwork for future research.

One of Rhine's most significant contributions was the use of statistical and laboratory methods for ascertaining the existence of what was now referred to as psi (a more neutral replacement for the loaded term 'paranormal'). The Zener card guessing experiment, developed by Rhine's colleague Dr. Karl Zener (1903-1964), is a good example of this new statistical methodology in action. Zener cards come in decks of twenty-five, consisting of five sets of cards, each set with its own easily recognisable symbol: five cards with a star, five with a wave, five with a circle, five with a square, and five with a cross. Research participants are then asked to guess, without seeing the deck, which cards the experimenter is holding up. Over the course of twenty-five cards it would be expected that, by chance alone, a participant would successfully guess the correct card five times out of twenty-five. Any number of correct guesses above the five expected by chance would, therefore, be a significant result suggesting an active selection of the correct card, rather than a random guess. This experimental method was particularly successful and quickly became a standard parapsychological tool.[143]

More recent parapsychological research has expanded on the statistical methods pioneered by Rhine and his colleagues, with the use of Random Number Generators (RNGs) in experiments being a particularly good example. RNGs are electronic devices that generate completely random numbers, without any pattern whatsoever, which are then projected through a visual display, usually using flashing lights. They were first employed in parapsychological research by the physicist Helmut Schmidt (1928-2011) in the 1970s. Schmidt asked his research participants to try to mentally influence red and green flashing lights on a screen, controlled by RNGs, through willing either the red or the green light to flash more frequently. If the participant was able to influence the flashing of the lights, a pattern would become apparent in the numbers generated by the RNG. Such patterns would be interpreted as indicating that an active process of selection had taken place, influencing the outcome of the RNG and thus suggesting some form of psychokinesis (PK), or influence of mind on matter. Schmidt reported a hit rate of between 1-2% higher than chance alone. Two meta-analyses of RNG experiments published in 2006, one by Radin and Nelson (who analysed the results from 515 separate studies), and the other by Bosch, Steinkamp and Boller, (who analysed the results from 380 separate studies) found an overall positive result of a small, but statistically significant, effect. Radin and Nelson interpreted these finds as indicative of psi, while Bosch *et al.* preferred to resort to more mundane explanations.[144] Nevertheless, such a positive effect certainly demands further investigation.

The ganzfeld experiment (from the German for 'whole field'), is one of the most frequently replicated experiments in parapsychology's repertoire. It was developed by the German Gestalt psychologist Wolfgang Metzger (1899-1979) as a means to promote endogenous mental imagery in his research subjects. The technique was later adopted and developed by parapsychologists in the 1970s because of growing evidence that telepathic, and other extrasensory experiences, are often associated with internal mental imagery. The experimental procedure initiates altered states of consciousness in participants by means of simulated sensory deprivation, achieved by placing halved ping pong balls over the participants' eyes, and playing pink noise through headphones while they are bathed in red light. Standardising the sensory input of participants creates a greater potential for endogenously generated mental imagery by shifting the attention away from the external world and onto internal processes. During these periods of introspection it is hypothesised that the participant will be more open to psi mediated sources of information.

In a standard ganzfeld experiment, then, two participants are separated into different rooms. One participant performs the role of 'sender,' attempting to send mental information to the 'receiver,' who attempts to pick up on what is being sent, while experiencing an altered state of consciousness. Dean Radin, a psi researcher at the Institute of Noetic Sciences, has conducted a meta-analysis (a statistical procedure designed to reveal the significance of experimental effects over many experiments) of 88 ganzfeld experiments carried out between 1974 and 2004, and revealed a combined hit rate of 32%, a significant result above the chance expectation of 25%. This 32% hit rate means that over the course of 3,145 trials in 88 experiments the receivers correctly identified the targets 1,008 times.[145] Of course, as with any evidence for the existence of psi, many sceptics have not been entirely convinced by the ganzfeld protocol. Meta-analyses like Radin's have also been criticised. Sceptics argue that the apparent positive effect must be due to methodological flaws in experimental design, combined with the selective reporting of experiments with positive results. As in the case of the RNG experiments, however, the fact that there are apparent positive effects at all demands that we take this research seriously.[146]

Interestingly, some of the best experimental evidence for ESP was gathered during experiments with sleeping participants at the Maimonides Dream Laboratory in New York by Stanley Krippner and Montague Ullman (1916-2008) in the 1960s and 1970s. Krippner and Ullman used EEG (electroencephalograph) devices to monitor the brain activity of sleeping participants. While the participants slept, a sender would attempt to convey specific images to the sleeping receiver. When the EEG devices showed that the receiver was in REM (rapid eye movement) sleep, which is associated with dreaming, the researchers woke them and asked them to describe their dreams in as much detail as possible. The next day the receivers would be asked to select the image that most resembled what they had seen in their dreams from a set of twelve different images. Independent judges would then compare the receiver's descriptions to the images. These studies continued for sixteen years, and showed a combined hit rate of 63% above the chance expectation of 50%, thus suggesting a genuine psi effect associated with the dream state.[147]

A classic parapsychological study, conducted by psychologist Dr. Gertrude Schmeidler (1912-2009) in the 1940s, revealed the important role played by the mindset and personal beliefs of individuals in the successful demonstration of psi in the laboratory. Using students at the City University of New York, Schmeidler developed a questionnaire to explore students' beliefs in psi abilities. Those who possessed a strong belief in psi were called 'sheep' and those who were highly sceptical of psi were labeled 'goats.' Following the questionnaire Schmeidler conducted a series of simple psi tests, using Zener cards (as developed by J.B. Rhine), she then compared the results of these experiments with the data from her sheep/goat questionnaire. Interestingly, Schmeidler found that those participants categorised as sheep (that is strong believers in the existence of psi), scored significantly in the psi tests (approximately 0.4% above chance), while those with a sceptical, unbelieving, attitude towards psi scored in the negative (approximately 0.3% below chance).[149] Schmeidler's findings appeared to suggest, therefore, that psi abilities are stronger, and more prevalent, amongst those who believe strongly in the existence of psi, and weak (if not negative), in those with a highly sceptical, non-believing, attitude. Schmeidler's initial research has been further expanded by more recent research.[150] Lawrence published a paper in 1993 reporting the results of a meta-analysis of 73 sheep/goat studies conducted between 1947-1993.[151] The meta-analysis demonstrated that positive results in psi tests are most often associated with those who believe in the existence of psi, while negative effects are more frequently associated with sceptical participants.

Extrasensory Perception and Psychokinesis

By the mid-twentieth century parapsychology had seemingly revealed two essential paranormal processes: Extrasensory Perception (ESP) and Psychokinesis (PK). The term 'extrasensory perception,' was first employed by J.B. Rhine to refer to the types of phenomena he was observing in his laboratory at Duke University. ESP can be regarded as a coverall term for a variety of different phenomena including:

1) Telepathy: referring to mind-to-mind communication through means other than the known human senses.

2) Clairvoyance: referring to the ability to gain information about an object, person, location or physical event through means other than the known human senses.

3) Precognition: referring to the acquisition in the present of information from the future which could not have been gained through any normal means of information transfer.

4) Retrocognition: referring to the acquisition in the present of information from the past which could not have been gained through any normal means of information transfer.

Today these different phenomena are subsumed under the broad category of psi, a term which Social Psychologist Daryl Bem defines as 'anomalous processes of information or energy transfer that are currently unexplained in terms of known physical or biological mechanisms.'[152] All of the phenomena we have just mentioned are concerned with processes of *information* transfer, psychokinesis (PK), however, is a term used to refer to processes of *energy* transfer, and more specifically the ability of consciousness to influence physical matter.

PK effects are often split into two categories micro-PK, referring to the influence of consciousness on, for example, random number generators (RNG), or other electronic equipment, and macro-PK, referring to the influence of consciousness on larger objects, from dice in the case of the dice rolling experiments conducted by J.B. Rhine, or the movement of tables in the case of traditional Spiritualist table-tipping seances. PK is now also the go-to explanation for parapsychologists studying the so-called poltergeist (noisy ghost) phenomenon. Poltergeist cases are characterised by intense physical disturbances, including, for example, the spontaneous levitation of objects of varying sizes, bright flashes of light, loud banging sounds, and so on. As the word 'poltergeist' implies, it used to be assumed that such phenomena were caused by disembodied spirits, but in the 1950s parapsychologist William G. Roll (1926-2012) put forward the hypothesis that the anomalous physical phenomena that occur during poltergeist outbreaks were the result of large scale psychokinesis, or what Roll called 'recurrent spontaneous psychokinesis' (RSPK). Roll noticed over the course of his investigations that poltergeist phenomena usually occurred within the close proximity of a particular individual, known as the focus, and that more often than not this individual was young and going through puberty. The poltergeist activity was, therefore, interpreted as an outward expression of emotional angst, mediated through psychokinesis.

The work of parapsychologist Kenneth Batcheldor (1921-1988) also has relevance to understanding the nature of PK. Batcheldor conducted experimental research with sitter-groups working with the classical Spiritualist table tipping phenomenon. During table tipping sessions members of the group sit around a table with their hands resting gently on its surface. After a period of relaxation and concentration the table begins to move, lifting up and down, rocking back and forth, and occasionally fully levitating above the ground. Members of the group will often ask the table to answer their questions on the assumption that the movements of the table are produced by an invisible intelligence. Batcheldor found that the movements of the table were considerably stronger when the sitter-group was composed of those who held a belief in the reality of the paranormal, just as Schmeidler had found in her sheep/goat ESP studies. But Batcheldor also noticed that what was most important in the production of large scale PK phenomena was not the long-term belief of the sitters, but rather their instant belief, which occurs at the time of the PK event itself. The important point is, therefore, that participants must believe in psi at the moment that PK is possible if psychokinetic phenomena are to manifest.[153] This finding led Batcheldor to an appreciation of the role that trickery can play in the manifestation of genuine psi phenomena. It was found that the deliberate faking of PK effects (referred to as 'artifacts'), at the start of experimental sessions assisted in the manifestation of genuine psychokinetic effects. Batcheldor reasoned that the artifacts led participants to believe that their efforts were successful (even if they were not), which boosted their 'instant belief,' which in turn led to stronger PK effects.

Although it seems reasonable to try to separate ESP and PK into different categories of phenomena - one dealing with information and the other with energy - it is theoretically difficult to make such clear-cut distinctions. It is much more likely, for example, that such faculties operate simultaneously and interdependently with one another. Parapsychologists Michael Thalbourne (1955-2010) and Lance Storm have suggested that the 'ESP-PK dichotomy is untenable,' and instead argue in favour of what they term the psychopractic hypothesis. They define psychopraxia (a term derived from the Greek - *psyche* meaning 'self' and *prattein* meaning 'to accomplish), as 'the self bringing about goals endosomatically in the mind-body complex and exosomatically in the wider world.' In other words, both ESP and PK are aspects of the same process of interaction between consciousness and the physical world.[154]

Mediumship Research

Much of the early work in psychical research was centered on the investigation of spirit mediumship and the possibility of the survival of consciousness after death - largely motivated by the popularity of Spiritualism. In the late nineteenth century it was physical mediumship that consumed the attention of psychical researchers. Psychologist John Klimo provides a fairly standard definition of physical mediumship as the purported ability of certain mediums to 'channel unknown energies that affect the physical environment in ways that can be directly experienced by persons other than the channel.'[155] Manifestations of these 'unknown energies' can take a variety of different forms including: the levitation and manipulation of physical objects (such as knocks and raps, table levitation, and so on); the production of anomalous environmental changes (such as breezes and unusual drops in room temperature); the generation of so-called 'spirit-lights'; the movement of physical objects into and out of the séance room ('apports'), and the materialization of ectoplasmic forms (manifestations of limbs, heads or, occasionally, whole bodies from a mysterious semi-physical substance exuded from the bodies of mediums), amongst others.[156] Such phenomena are, by their very physical nature, particularly controversial even within the parapsychological community.

Many physical mediums were exposed as fraudulent by members of the SPR, but there were some exceptions who continued to demonstrate seemingly baffling physical phenomena, even under the strictest control conditions. D.D. Home, as we have already seen, was one of these. Another such baffling medium was the Italian Eusapia Palladino (1854-1918). Indeed, Nobel prize winning physiologist Prof. Charles Richet (1850-1935) first coined the term 'ectoplasm' in 1894 in reference to observations of anomalous materialised limbs during experiments with Palladino. Research into physical mediumship, however, was notoriously difficult. Because of the association with fraudulence, physical mediumship research became increasingly disreputable as the twentieth century dawned. As a consequence there was a shift in the focus of research away from physical mediumship towards mental mediumship, which many researchers considered to provide better evidence for the survival of consciousness. Mental mediumship itself consists of two strands - one in which visions and messages are subjectively perceived by the medium, and the other when the body of the medium is overtaken by different spirit personalities.

The biggest star of early mental mediumship research was undoubtedly Leonora Piper (1857-1950), often referred to simply as Mrs. Piper.[157] Mrs. Piper would go into a trance state during which so-called 'spirit controls' would communicate with sitters. Her main control called himself Dr. Phinuit and claimed to have been a medical doctor in France when alive on the Earth Plane. Despite the efforts of psychical researchers, such as William James (1842-1910), however, no record of a Dr. Phinuit was ever found in the records of the medical school he claimed to have attended. This led psychical theorists like Eleanor Sidgwick (1845-1936) to conclude that these alleged spirit controls were really portions of the medium's own consciousness somehow separated from her normal everyday waking consciousness (dissociated). Nevertheless, Piper's controls were able to provide a great deal of accurate and verifiable information, even under the strictest experimental conditions (when invited to stay in Britain by the SPR, Mrs. Piper was constantly monitored by private detectives to ensure that no foul-play was at hand).

Mental mediumship research continues today, with increasingly stringent experimental controls. The work of Dr. Julie Beischel and her colleagues and the Windbridge Research Center perhaps representing the current pinnacle of methodological rigour in mediumship research.[158] Although controversial, the findings of the Windbridge researchers are suggestive of the ability of certain individuals to receive accurate information concerning the deceased loved-ones of research participants, even under stringent quadruple blinded experimental conditions. Such findings are certainly interesting and demand further investigation.

The evidence from mediumship research is subject to two primary interpretations, additional to the usual sceptical interpretation of fraudulent 'cold reading.' The first, and perhaps most controversial, is the survival hypothesis, which suggests that the accuracy of the information received by mediums results from actual communication with discarnate spirits. The second interpretation is the super-psi hypothesis, which holds that the information retrieved during mediumship demonstrations is not received from discarnate spirits, but rather is the result of highly attuned ESP of one form or another. This is an ongoing problem in mediumship research.

Near-Death and Out-of-Body Experiences

Not all parapsychologists focus their research efforts on laboratory experiments, especially when it comes to the investigation of phenomena that occur spontaneously, such as Near-Death Experiences (NDEs) and Out-of-Body Experiences (OBEs). Some of the earliest forays into serious out-of-body experience research were conducted by the psychical researcher Dr. Hereward Carrington (1880-1958), most notably in books co-authored with the astral projector Sylvan Muldoon (1903-1969). Muldoon and Carrington noted many intriguing similarities between reports of OBEs that strongly suggested they were dealing with a real phenomenon.[159]

The American businessman Robert A. Monroe (1915-1995) was another early populariser of the out-of-body experience. In the 1960s, Monroe began to experience regular and uncontrollable OBEs, during which he discovered that he had a non-physical 'second body' that occupied an apparently immaterial plane of existence. Over the course of further investigation and practice he was able to refine his abilities to control this non-physical body and to induce his out-of-body state at will. This provided Monroe with the perfect opportunity to conduct a thorough exploration of this hitherto hidden world. His descriptions, therefore, provide interesting data for comparison with the spirit world conceptions of other cultures and traditions. Monroe separated this second world into distinct locales, what he refers to as Locale I is described as:

> ...the most believable. It consists of people and places that actually do exist in the material, well known world at the very moment of the experiment. It is the world represented to us by our physical senses which most of us are fairly sure does exist. Visits to Locale I... should not contain strange beings, events, or places. Unfamiliar, perhaps, but not strange and unknown.

This idea seems very much like the ancient Egyptian notion of Sekhet Aaru: a spirit world that essentially resembles the world of the living in its main features (see Chapter Two). Locale II, by contrast is described as a

> ...non-material environment with laws of motion and matter only remotely related to the physical world. It is an immensity whose bounds

are unknown...and has depth and dimension incomprehensible to the finite, conscious mind. In this vastness lie all the aspects we attribute to heaven and hell, which are but part of Locale II. It is inhabited, if that is the word, by entities with various degrees of intelligence with whom communication is possible.

In this second Locale thought is primary: 'As you think, so you are.' Unlike in Locale I, vehicles are not required as movement is achieved via thought. Monroe speculates that Locale II is the natural home of the second body. Locale III, the third and final non-physical realm explored by Monroe in his second body, is described as a 'physical matter world almost identical to our own. The natural environment is the same. There are trees, houses, cities, people, artefacts, and all the appurtenances of a reasonably civilized society. There are homes, families, businesses, and people work for a living. There are roads on which vehicles travel. There are railroads and trains.'[160]

The first systematic study of the phenomenology of the NDE was undertaken by Dr. Raymond Moody in his classic study *Life after Life*, first published in 1975.[161] Based on in-depth interviews with 150 people who reported unusual experiences while clinically dead, Moody developed a schema of recurrent themes in the average NDE. These include:

1) An overwhelming feeling of peace and well-being, including freedom from pain.
2) The impression of being located outside one's physical body.
3) Floating or drifting through darkness, sometimes described as a tunnel.
4) Becoming aware of a golden light.
5) Encountering and perhaps communicating with a 'being of light.'
6) Having a rapid succession of visual images of one's past.
7) Experiencing another world of much beauty.

Although NDEs do not always follow Moody's schema, many of the characteristic features he described do appear to be fairly standard in experiencer accounts. In addition to the kind of phenomenological approach employed by Moody, more recent NDE researchers have focused on attempting to find veridical evidence that the experiencer really did leave their body while experiencing the NDE. A notable example, which appears to describe a veridical NDE, was reported by

Penny Sartori, Paul Badham and Peter Fenwick.[162] As part of a five-year prospective study at Morriston Hospital in Swansea, South Wales, Penny Sartori placed brightly coloured symbols out of view on top of cardiac monitors in hospital rooms in the hope that they might be seen from an out-of-body perspective in the event of an NDE. In the case reported by Sartori, Badham and Fenwick the near-death experiencer was not able to describe the symbols that had been placed on top of his cardiac monitor, but was able to provide a great deal of verifiable information concerning the events that took place in the room while he was 'deeply unconscious.' Such accounts are not uncommon in the NDE literature and, although they have been subject to a great deal of sceptical criticism, do seem to provide tantalising evidence for the existence of veridical out-of-body experiences, as well as the possibility of the survival of consciousness after death, that begs for further investigation.

The two primary competing explanations of the NDE experience suggest either that the Near-Death Experience is a natural experience associated with the dying brain, as expounded by psychologist Susan Blackmore,[163] and that the Near-Death Experience provides a glimpse of consciousness existing beyond the confines of the brain. The debate is still raging.

A Note on Proponents and Sceptics

Much of the research cited in this short chapter comes from so-called psi-proponents, that is from researchers who emphasise the psi hypothesis as the best model for describing their experimental data. There is, however, always another side to the story, especially when it comes to the kinds of 'extraordinary' phenomena reported by parapsychologists. For the sake of brevity I have not included full accounts of the sceptical criticisms levelled against the experiments discussed here, but suffice to say that the sceptical contribution to parapsychology has been, and continues to be, an important one, helping to refine the protocols for experiments and resulting in parapsychology becoming one of the most methodologically rigorous disciplines.[164] It is strongly advised, therefore, that the interested reader explore the sceptical literature alongside the parapsychological literature in order to develop a deeper, more nuanced, appreciation of the contemporary debate.

CHAPTER 7

TOWARDS AN ANTHROPOLOGY OF THE PARANORMAL

~

A ll of this leads us towards an approach to the study of paranormal experiences, phenomena and beliefs that integrates the findings and methodologies of both anthropology and parapsychology. This is not necessarily a new idea, having precedents throughout the history of anthropology,[165] and beginning with the efforts of Andrew Lang in the late nineteenth century to promote what he termed comparative psychical research. Lang saw distinct similarities, across both time and space, in narrative accounts of paranormal experiences and phenomena, which led him to conclude that something more than mere 'hallucination' and 'trickery' was going on. He wrote, for instance, of similarities in descriptions of apparent spirit manifestations cross-culturally:

> ... from the Australians...in the bush, who hear raps when the spirits come, to ancient Egypt, and thence to Greece, and last, in our own time, and in a London suburb, similar experiences, real or imaginary, are explained by the same hypothesis. No 'survival' can be more odd and striking, none more illustrative of the permanence, in human nature, of certain elements.[166]

Lang considered these cross-cultural similarities to be particularly important observations (not least because they seemed to provide independent, cross-cultural, evidence for certain phenomena), and as such was critical of both his contemporaries in anthropology and members of the Society for Psychical Research (of which he was also a member), for not sharing ideas and insights: the anthropologists were unwilling to take the literature of psychical research seriously, and the psychical researchers were unwilling to investigate accounts of ostensibly paranormal phenomena documented in the ethnographic literature. It wasn't until the twentieth century that a real cross-pollination of ideas began to take shape.

In 1968 a posthumously published book by Italian philosopher and anthropologist Ernesto de Martino (1908–1965) presented a synthesis of the findings of anthropology and parapsychology. One of the most significant observations de Martino made was that the laboratory investigation of psi involves a complete reduction of the emotional and environmental contexts within which psi experiences naturally occur. He wrote that 'in the laboratory, the drama of the dying man who appears...to a relative or friend, is reduced to an oft repeated experiment – one that tries to transmit to the mind of a subject the image of a playing card, chosen at random.' This, he suggests, represents 'an almost complete reduction of the historical stimulus that is at work in the purely spontaneous occurrence of such phenomena.'[167] In other words; the drama of real life is ignored in the laboratory experiment, and it is precisely at this juncture that the ethnographic methodology of anthropology succeeds in illuminating the nature of the paranormal: through documenting its occurrence in the midst of the social drama that allows psi to manifest in its most elaborate forms (as we saw in Chapter Five). De Martino's contribution to the development of an anthropological approach was an important one, though it is often overlooked because many of his books have not been translated into English.

Significant contributions to this developing trend in anthropology were later published in the book *Extrasensory Ecology*, edited by Joseph K. Long in 1974,[168] inspired partly by Long's own unusual experiences while conducting fieldwork in Jamaica, and in an important edited volume published by the Parapsychology Foundation in the same year.[169] These books were groundbreaking in their presentation of a seriously reasoned anthropological evaluation of the evidence from parapsychology, and the implications of this data for theory development in anthropology, and were the seeds for what would eventually emerge as the anthropology of consciousness.

The Society for the Anthropology of Consciousness (SAC) was established in 1989 as a member of the American Anthropological Association, and has subsequently developed as an anthropological sub-discipline with a particular stated interest in states of consciousness and consciousness studies, shamanic, religious, and spiritual traditions, psychoactive substances, philosophical, symbolic, and linguistic studies, and anomalous experiences.[170] The roots of the anthropology of consciousness go right back to the early pioneering work of the likes of E.B. Tylor and Andrew Lang, whose interests in the experiential origins of supernatural beliefs were clear precursors to the movement.

The anthropology of consciousness also has roots in slightly more recent trends in intellectual thought, including specifically transpersonal psychology and (slightly later), transpersonal anthropology.[171] Transpersonal anthropologist Charles Laughlin defines transpersonalism as 'a movement in science towards seeing experiences had in life that somehow go beyond the boundaries of ordinary ego-consciousness as data.'[172] Such experiences may include any number of ostensibly paranormal experiences and altered states of consciousness, as well as including more mundane (though not necessarily any less meaningful) experiences such as dreaming, *deja vu*, coincidences and so on.

Typical methods in the anthropology of consciousness include active and immersive participation in rituals and other performances, and a deliberate attempt to attain the states of consciousness that are important to the particular society under investigation, this might include, for example, consuming psychoactive substances, and participating in other forms of consciousness alteration. Indeed, Charles Laughlin has defined the transpersonal anthropologist as one who is 'capable of participating in transpersonal experience; that is, capable of both attaining whatever extraordinary experiences and phases of consciousness that enrich the religious system, and relating these experiences to...patterns of symbolism, cognition and practice found in religions and cosmologies all over the planet.'[173]

Other approaches to the study of the transpersonal and paranormal within an anthropological framework have also developed. Anthropologist Patric Giesler, for example, has proposed a methodology, which he terms psi-in-process, for investigating the social and cultural factors involved in the manifestation of psi phenomena, as and when they occur in the field. Such an approach attempts to overcome the limitations of classical laboratory based parapsychological research by conducting experiments in the field, as de Martino suggested, with minimal reduction of the natural environmental setting. Giesler's own research has, for example, investigated psi phenomena in the context of Brazilian Umbanda spirit possession rituals. Giesler's approach takes a significant step away from the more traditional bracketing out of questions of ontology in phenomenological and social-scientific approaches to supernatural beliefs, he writes:

> ... one of the purposes of anthropology is to explain the ontology, development, and function of the beliefs, practices, and claims of magico-religious experiences ... it should assume that psi could exist and then proceed etically on that assumption.[174]

Another particularly important book in bringing about a new anthropological approach to the paranormal, and in particular in taking the extraordinary experiences of ethnographers engaged in fieldwork seriously, was David E. Young and Jean-Guy Goulet's *Being Changed by Cross-Cultural Encounters*, first published in 1994. In their introduction Young and Goulet suggest that their book attempts to do three important things:

> (1) provide personal accounts by anthropologists who have taken their informants' extraordinary experiences seriously or who have had extraordinary experiences themselves, (2) develop the beginnings of a theoretical framework which will help facilitate an understanding of such experiences, and (3) explore the issue of how such experiences can be conveyed and explained to a 'scientifically-oriented' audience in such a way that they are not automatically dismissed without a fair hearing.[175]

A more recent development is the notion of 'paranthropology'[176] - a term first coined by the Linguist Roger W. Wescott (1925-2000) in Joseph K. Long's book *Extrasensory Ecology*. Anthropologist Fabian Graham differentiates paranthropology from more traditional approaches to the anthropology of religion according to the way in which the two approaches relate to the objects of religious and paranormal beliefs. While the anthropology of religion has tended to focus primarily on systems of religious belief, bracketing out or negating the reality of the objects of such beliefs, a paranthropological approach accepts the possibility that the objects of supernatural beliefs may have some form of independent ontological reality. He writes:

... paranthropology [defines] itself in relation to the phenomena themselves, and not (in relation) to the belief systems, scientific or religious, that have evolved to support the phenomena.[177]

Paranthropology, therefore, takes a bold step in attempting to interpret supernatural systems of belief from the perspective of those who subscribe to them. In studies of spirit mediumship, for example, a paranthropologist will take seriously their informants beliefs about, and experiences of, spirits in an attempt to gain a more rounded appreciation of what such beliefs and experiences mean. Further to this, and in line with the immersive approach recommended by Edith Turner, and transpersonal anthropologists like Charles Laughlin, the paranothropologist will attempt to participate, as far as possible, in the rites, rituals and performances under study in order to develop an 'insider' perspective. A truly rounded study of spirit possession, for instance, cannot be complete without an appreciation of the experiential component, which certainly plays a central role in the development of traditions of practice and belief. Such an approach might also come under what parapsychologist David Luke calls first-person parapsychology.[178]

Parapsychology's Main Findings and Their Relation to Anthropology

A criticism that is often levelled against parapsychology is that over the last 130 years, since the Society for Psychical Research (SPR) was established in 1882, the discipline has been unable to formulate any definite conclusions with regard to the nature of the phenomena it investigates. Strictly speaking, however, this is not the case. Indeed, parapsychological research has resulted in the development of several key concepts, including the significant role of altered states of consciousness, mindset and culture in the production of psi phenomena. This last section will present some of parapsychology's main findings with an aim to demonstrating how they can help illuminate the ethnographic data, as well as showing how ethnographic data can supplement parapsychological research.

Altered States of Consciousness

Potentially, parapsychology's most important finding is the recognition of the ubiquitous role of altered states of consciousness in the experience of the paranormal.[179] Frederic Myers, a founding member of the Society for Psychical Research, was well aware of this fact. In his posthumously published *Human Personality and its Survival of Bodily Death*,[180] Myers devotes entire chapters to discussions of various altered states of consciousness, including somnambulism and sleep, which he considered to be intimately related to the types of experiences reported by mediums. Early psychical researchers also recognised the fact that many paranormal experiences occurred during sleep, and near-sleep, states (sleep being, as we have already seen, perhaps the most common form of altered consciousness). The evidence from the Ganzfeld studies, and from the Sleep ESP studies conducted by Stanley Krippner in the 1970s also point towards the central role of altered states in the mediation of psi experiences.

The significant role of altered states of consciousness with regard to psi[181] is also attested to in the anthropological literature, most notably in the literature on shamanism and spirit possession. As we have already seen, the anthropologist Erika Bourguignon provides ample evidence that altered states of consciousness are near universal, and that in the majority of cases they are thought to provide direct access to the spiritual realm.[182] Paranthropologists should, therefore, be aware of the role of altered states of consciousness, and techniques for the alteration of consciousness, in their investigations of paranormal beliefs, practices and experiences in the field.

Mindset and Cultural Setting

When we consider the types of paranormal experiences recounted by anthropologists engaged in ethnographic fieldwork (such as those discussed in the previous chapter), Schmeidler's sheep/goat study, and Batcheldor's experiments with table-tipping (as discussed in the previous chapter), prove particularly insightful. The types of paranormal phenomena reported by anthropologists are far more intense than those investigated by parapsychologists in laboratory settings: Bruce Grindal's experience of a corpse re-animating during a divination session,[183] or Edith Turner's witnessing the extraction of a malevolent spirit during a healing ceremony,[184] are of a much greater magnitude of weirdness to the psi effects documented in the laboratory.

There are, however, significant differences between the contexts in which such phenomena arise in the field, and in the laboratory. Perhaps chief amongst these differences is the culture within which they occur. Grindal and Turner's experiences arose while immersed in cultures that both expected and intended such phenomena to occur, while laboratory based psi experiments are conducted in a culture that is, on the whole, averse to the notion of paranormal phenomena. If Schmeidler and Batcheldor's ideas about the impact of belief on psi functioning are correct, then the dominant attitudes within a given culture must surely have a significant effect on the strength of psi phenomena, and the forms in which they manifest. Levi-Strauss sums this up nicely in a discussion of the efficacy of magical cursing and healing. He writes:

> There is, therefore, no reason to doubt the efficacy of certain magical practices. But at the same time we see that the efficacy of magic implies a belief in magic. The latter has three complimentary aspects: first, the sorcerer's belief in the effectiveness of his techniques; second, the patient's or victim's belief in the sorcerer's power; and, finally, the faith and expectations of the group, which constantly act as a sort of gravitational field within which the relationship between sorcerer and bewitched is located and defined.[185]

Psi and Culture

Psi and culture appear, therefore, to be intimately interconnected because they are either products, or aspects, of consciousness. The field of transcultural psychiatry, being the study of mental illness across different cultures, provides a useful illustration of the influence of culture on consciousness (and vice versa). Transcultural psychiatry recognises that illness is a culturally constructed category, and that different cultures identify illnesses in different ways. In other words, different cultures possess different types and expressions of mental illness. There are, therefore, many so-called culture-bound disorders,[186] with symptoms that only occur within particular cultural contexts. A classic example of just such a culture-bound disorder is an unusual Malaysian ailment known as *koro*, which refers to a particular disorder, recognised in the DSM-V as a culture-bound illness, whereby a man becomes convinced that his genitals are shrinking, or retracting into his body. Koro is a specific culturally recognised symptom of underlying mental illness. The physical symptoms are the outward expression of disorders of consciousness. The European disease known as hysteria during the nineteenth century also provides a good example. Many of the symptoms observed in hysteric patients simply do not occur in the present day, examples include rigidity of the body, convulsions, faintness, nervousness, sexual desire, insomnia, and many others, but at the time were culturally recognised bodily expressions of underlying mental illness.[187]

I am not trying to suggest that psi phenomena are the product of mental illness, rather I am suggesting that both psi and mental illness are aspects of consciousness and that their expression is fundamentally affected by the expectations, categories, and beliefs of the people experiencing them. Just as the symptoms of mental illness vary across cultures, so too do expressions of psi.

Conclusions

The data presented in this book appear to coalesce into something resembling a coherent model: a model that emphasises psi as a feature of consciousness and that shows the role of culture in modulating the expression of psi, perhaps something like a filter or lens. I feel that it is important, however, to highlight the incompleteness of this model, particularly in relation to our relative ignorance of the fundamental processes involved. It is also important to note that the factors outlined here (the role of belief and intention, the use of altered states of consciousness, and so on), are only a few of potentially countless other factors that might be involved. A great deal more research, both in the laboratory and in the field is needed.[188] Nevertheless, these initial observations are important and should help to point us in the direction of an anthropological approach to the paranormal that is inclusive of the data and research methods of parapsychology, while also preserving the ecological conditions that anthropology is best suited to study.

In concluding this short book, it is my hope that the reader will have found something of interest in the preceding pages, and that they might be inspired to further their own inquiries into the nature of the paranormal, not from a culturally isolated perspective, but rather from an holistic cross-cultural perspective. This, combined with a multi-disciplinary approach, I believe, is the way forward: it is our route towards engaging and understanding the mysteries of the supernatural, and to providing us with insights into the processes of nature and the meaning of human existence.

AFTERWORD

DAVID LUKE

~

My own suspicion is that the Universe is not only queerer than we suppose, but queerer than we can suppose.

—British geneticist and
evolutionary biologist, J.B.S. Haldane[189]

S tudying the anthropology of the supernatural is important in a number of ways. First, by studying the supernatural from an anthropological perspective it provides an opportunity to see what practices, beliefs and experiences people have in different cultures, and unsurprisingly this reveals a uniqueness of some experiences, such as *koro*, and yet a commonality across cultures of many other phenomena. The phenomena found to be common to many cultures, although they may have certain differences in content, includes near-death experiences, out-of-body experiences, sleep paralysis, psi in all its many manifestations, apparitions and mediumship, all of which are researched in the developed world under the auspices of parapsychology. However, it is only from the cross-cultural study of such phenomena that we can establish that they are universal to humans everywhere, even though not everyone experiences them, and this gives us special insight by indicating that such phenomena are not just culture bound. Where the anthropological study of these phenomena really becomes interesting is in the different beliefs that individuals in different cultures have for explaining them, often at odds with the dominant Western scientific viewpoint (which usually considers all paranormal phenomena as some kind of deception), which itself is just another belief. Not all scientists are of this usual dismissive opinion though, and parapsychologists and others open to the possibility, at least, of genuine anomalous phenomena demonstrate that an open-minded and scientific approach need not be conflicted, indeed – much like the approach of this book – it would seem a more honest way to address these experiences.

Ideally, an anthropological approach can also provide insights from a non-ethnocentric position, so that cultural bias is minimised in interpreting supernatural phenomena and beliefs, although in reality bias can never be totally bypassed and anthropology has many times been guilty of ethnocentrism, especially the further back in the past we go. However, breaking through the cultural divide through participant observation, and yet – through a delicate balance – maintaining the intellectual rigour of the field can allow for insights into the supernatural that utilise both insider and outsider perspectives. Indeed, this book is to be celebrated for advocating such an approach, one that at least initially respects the phenomena from the perspective of those reporting it, that is treating it "as if" it is real, and then seeing what ensues, rather than dismissing the phenomena as not real from the outset.

This fair and reasoned approach to the supernatural in other cultures is typified by the recent emergence of paranthropology as a renewed anthropological approach to the paranormal. Paranthropology is a rejuvenation of the transpersonal anthropology that arose in the 1970s, largely as a backlash to intellectual prejudice against honest and open reporting of paranormal phenomena by anthropologists at that time. Paranthropology offers a fresh approach to the phenomena in that it attempts to avoid making a priori judgements about the reality, or not, of different experiences and beliefs, and instead aims to explore the phenomena in the spirit of Joseph K. Long, in that, 'a persistent ignoring of the relevancy of parapsychology in anthropology is nothing less than scientistic ethnocentricism.'[190] Indeed the very acceptance of these phenomena as experiences at least worthy of scientific consideration harks back to the writings of the father of American psychology, William James, who in his posthumous treatise on 'Radical Empiricism' entreated researchers to include all experience under the rubric of science. Celebrating the centenary of that book in 2012, we are reminded by William James that, 'to be radical an empiricism must neither admit into its construction any element that is not directly experienced, nor exclude from them [sic] any element that is directly experienced.'[191] In keeping with James then we can be empirical in a radical way and approach the supernatural within anthropology with a broad scientific perspective that is at least open to the possibility of paranormal phenomena, and in such a manner avoid the ethnocentrism of earlier, and indeed some contemporary, researchers. This book is an excellent step in that direction.

ABOUT THE AUTHOR

Jack Hunter, Ph.D., is an Honorary Research Fellow with the Alister Hardy Religious Experience Research Centre and a member of the Sophia Centre, both at the University of Wales Trinity Saint David, and is Research Fellow with the Parapsychology Foundation, New York. He is the founder and editor of *Paranthropology: Journal of Anthropological Approaches to the Paranormal* and the author of *Engaging the Anomalous* (2018) and *Manifesting Spirits* (2020). He is the editor *of Strange Dimensions: A Paranthropology Anthology* (2015), *Damned Facts: Fortean Essays on Religion, Folklore and the Paranormal* (2016), *Greening the Paranormal: Exploring the Ecology of Extraordinary Experience* (2019), and co-editor with Dr. David Luke of *Talking with the Spirits: Ethnographies from Between the Worlds* (2014). He lives in the hills of Mid-Wales with his family.

REFERENCES

～

[1] Hunter, J. (2019). *Greening the Paranormal: Exploring the Ecology of Extraordinary Experience*. Milton Keynes: August Night Press.

[2] Hunter, J. (2020). *Manifesting Spirits: Anthropology, the Paranormal and Discarnate Entities*. London: Aeon Books.

[3] Hunter, J. (2016). *Damned Facts: Fortean Essays on Religion, Folklore and the Paranormal*. Paphos: Aporetic Press.

[4] Hunter, J. (2018). *Engaging the Anomalous: Collected Essays on Anthropology, the Paranormal, Mediumship and Extraordinary Experience*. Milton Keynes: August Night Press.

[5] Holbraad, M. & Pedersen, M. (2017). *The Ontological Turn: An Anthropological Exposition*. Cambridge: Cambridge University Press. (p. 11).

[6] Palecek, M. & Risjord, M. (2013). 'Relativism and the Ontological Turn within Anthropology.' *Philosophy of the Social Sciences*, Vol. 43, No. 1, pp. 3-23.

[7] Bartlett, R (2008). *The Natural and the Supernatural in the Middle Ages*. Cambridge: Cambridge University Press.

[8] Durkheim, E. (2008). *The Elementary Forms of Religious Life*. Oxford: Oxford University Press. (p. 28).

[9] Hume, D. (1993). *An Enquiry Concerning Human Understanding*. Cambridge: Hackett. (p. 77)

[10] Hunter, J. & Luke, D. (2014). *Talking With the Spirits: Ethnographies from Between the Worlds.* Brisbane: Daily Grail.

[11] Braude, S. (1997). *The Limits of Influence: Psychokinesis and the Philosophy of Science.* New York: University Press of America.

[12] Boyer, P. (2001). *Religion Explained: The Human Instincts that Fashion Gods, Spirits and Ancestors.* London: William Heinnemann. (pp. 2-3).

[13] Tylor, E. B. (1930). *Anthropology: An Introduction to the Study of Man and Civilization.* London: C.A. Watts and Co. Ltd.

[14] Durkheim, *The Elementary Forms of Religious Life.*

[15] Geertz, C. (1973). "Religion as a Cultural System." In C. Geertz, *The Interpretation of Cultures.* New York: Basic Books. (pp. 87-125).

[16] Smart, N. (1974). *The Religious Experience of Mankind.* London: Fontana.

[17] Evans-Prtichard, E.E. (1972). *Theories of Primitive Religion.* Oxford: Clarendon Press.

[18] Malinowski, B. (1948). *Magic, Science and Religion.* Boston: Beacon Press.

[19] Leach, E. (1970). *Levi-Strauss.* London: Fontana. p. 21.

[20] Guthrie, S. (1993). *Faces in the Clouds: A New Theory of Religion.* Oxford: Oxford University Press.

[21] Barrett, J. (2000). 'Exploring the natural foundation of religion.' *Trends in Cognitive Science,* Vol. 4, No. 1, pp. 29-34.

[22] Radcliffe-Brown, A.R. (1965). *Structure and Function in Primitive Society.* New York: The Free Press.

[23] James, W. (2004). *The Varieties of Religious Experience.* New York: Barnes & Noble.

[24] Otto, R. (1958). *The Idea of the Holy.* Oxford: Oxford University Press.

[25] Hufford, D.J. (1982). *The Terror that Comes in the Night: An Experience-Centered Study of Supernatural Assault Traditions.* Philadelphia: University of Pennsylvania Press.

[26] Lang, A. (1995). *Myth, Ritual and Religion Vol. I.* London: Senate.

[27] Turner, E.. (1998). *Experiencing Ritual: A New Interpretation of African Healing.* Philadelphia: University of Pennsylvania Press.

[28] Ackroyd, P. (2010). *The English Ghost: Spectres Through Time*. London: Random House.

[29] O'Connor, K.P. & Hallam, R.S. (2000). "Sorcery of the Self: The Magic of You." *Theory & Psychology*, Vol. 10, No. 2, pp. 238-264.

[30] Mauss, M. (1985). "A Category of the Human Mind: The Notion Of Person; The Notion of Self." In M. Carrithers, Collins, S. & Lukes, S., (eds.). *The Category of the Person: Anthropology, Philosophy, History*. Cambridge: Cambridge University Press. pp. 1-26.

[31] La Fontaine, J.S. (1985). "Person and Individual: Some Anthropological Reflections." In M. Carrithers, Collins, S. & Lukes, S. (eds.). *The Category of the Person: Anthropology, Philosophy, History*. Cambridge: Cambridge University Press. pp.123-140.

[32] Strathern, M. (1988). *The Gender of the Gift: Problems with Women and Problems with Society in Melanesia*. Berkeley: University of California Press.

[33] Budge, E.A.W. (1987). *Egyptian Religion: Egyptian Ideas of the Future Life*. St Ives: Arkana.

[34] Emmons, C. (1982). *Chinese Ghosts and ESP: A Study of Paranormal Beliefs and Experiences*. Metuchen: Scarecrow Press. (pp. 16-17).

[35] Malinowski, B. (1916). 'Baloma: The Spirits of the Dead in the Trobriand Islands.' *Journal of the Royal Anthropological Institute*, Vol. 46, pp. 353-430.

[36] Weiss, G. (1972). 'Campa Cosmology.' *Ethnology*, Vol. 11, No. 2, pp. 157-172.

[37] Hultkrantz, A. (1987). 'Diversity in Cosmology: The Case of the Wind River Shoshoni.' *Canadian Journal of Native Studies*, Vol. 7, No. 2, pp. 279-295.

[38] Luhrmann, T. (2012). *When God Talks Back: Understanding the American Evangelical Relationship with God*. New York: Knopf.

[39] Olson, C. (2011). *Religious Studies: Key Concepts*. London: Routledge.

[40] Steadman, L.B., Palmer, C.T. & Tilley, C.F. (1996). 'The Universality of Ancestor Worship.' *Ethnology*, Vol. 35, No. 1, pp. 63-76.

[41] Blackburn, S.H. (1985). 'Death and Deification: Folk Cults in Hinduism.' *History of Religions*, Vol. 24, No. 3, pp. 255-274.

[42] Harvey, G. (2005). *Animism: Respecting the Living World*. London: Hurst & Company.

[43] Hallowell, A.I. (2002) "Ojibwa Ontology, Behaviour, and World View." In G. Harvey (ed.) *Readings in Indigenous Religions*. London: Continuum. pp. 17-50.

[44] Viveiros de Castro, E. (1998). 'Cosmological Deixis and Amerindian Perspectivism.' *Journal of the Royal Anthropological Institute*, Vol. 4, No. 3, pp. 469-488.

[45] Abdel Hamid, D.M.S. (2014). 'A Chronological Study of the False Door Concept.' *Journal of the Association of Arab Universities for Tourism and Hospitality*, Vol. 18, No. 3, pp. 110-117.

[46] Brandes, S. (1998). 'The Day of the Dead, Halloween, and the Quest for Mexican National Identity.' *The Journal of American Folklore*, Vol. 111, No. 442, pp. 359-380.

[47] Waters, D. (2004). 'The Hungry Ghost Festival in Aberdeen Street, Hong Kong.' *Journal of the Royal Asiatic Society Hong Kong*, Vol. 44, pp. 41-55.

[48] Chan, M. (2012). "Bodies for the Gods: Image Worship in Chinese Popular Religion." In J. Bautista (ed.) *The Spirit of Things: Materiality and Religious Diversity in Southeast Asia*. New York: Cornell University Press. (pp. 197-215).

[49] Malinowski, B. (1916). 'Baloma: The Spirits of the Dead in the Trobriand Islands.' *Journal of the Royal Anthropological Institute*, Vol. 46, pp. 353-430.

[50] Bullard, T.E. (1989). "UFO Abduction Reports: The Supernatural Kidnap Narrative Returns in Technological Guise." *Journal of American Folklore*, Vol. 102, No. 404, pp. 147-170.

[51] Rojcewicz, P. M. (1986). "The Extraordinary Encounter Continuum Hypothesis and Its Implications for the Study of Belief Materials." *Folklore Forum*, Vol. 19, No. 2, pp. 131-152.

[52] Rojcewicz, P. M. (1986). "The Extraordinary Encounter Continuum Hypothesis and Its Implications for the Study of Belief Materials." Folklore Forum, Vol. 19, No. 2, pp. 131-152.

[53] Evans, H. (1987). *Gods, Spirits, Cosmic Guardians: Encounters With Non-Human Beings*. Wellingborough: The Aquarian Press. (p. 51-59).

[54] Adams, C. (2011). 'Psychedelics, Spirits and the Sacred Feminine: Communion as Cultural Critique.' *Paranthropology: Journal of Anthropological Approaches to the Paranormal*, Vol. 2, No. 3, pp. 49-52.

55 Strassman, R. (2001). *DMT: The Spirit Molecule*. Rochester: Park Street Press.

56 Wilson, R.A. (2000). *Cosmic Trigger: Final Secret of the Illuminati*. Tempe: New Falcon Publications.

57 Castaneda, C. (1976). *The Teachings of Don Juan: A Yaqui Way of Knowledge*. Harmondsworth: Penguin Books.

58 Luke, D. (2008). 'Disembodied Eyes Revisited: An Investigation into the Ontology of Entheogenic Entity Encounters.' *The Entheogen Review*, Vol. 7, No. 1, pp. 1-9.

59 Davies, O. (2011). *Paganism: A Very Short Introduction*. Oxford: Oxford University Press. (p. 7).

60 Bar-Yosef Mayer, D.E., Vandermeersh, B. & Bar-Yosef, O. (2009). 'Shells and ochre in Middle Paleolithic Qafzeh Cave, Israel: indications for modern behavior.' *Journal of Human Evolution*, Vol. 56, No. 3, pp. 307-314.

61 Lewis-Williams, D. & Clotte, J. (1998). 'The Mind in the Cave - The Cave in the Mind: Altered Consciousness in the Palaeolithic.' *Anthropology of Consciousness*, Vol. 9, No. 1, pp. 13-21.

62 Emmons, C. & Emmons, P. (2012). *Science and Spirit: Exploring the Limits of Consciousness*. Bloomington: iUniverse. (pp. 65-75).

63 Blackmore, S. (2005). *Consciousness: A Very Short Introduction*. Oxford: Oxford University Press. (p. 5).

64 Devereux, P. (2008). *The Long Trip: A Prehistory of Psychedelia*. Brisbane: Daily Grail Publishing.

65 Bourguignon, E. (1973). *Religion, Altered States of Consciousness and Social Change*. Columbus: Ohio State University Press.

66 Laughlin, C.D. (2012). "Transpersonal Anthropology: What is it, and What are the Problems we Face Doing It?" In J. Hunter (ed.) *Paranthropology: Anthropological Approaches to the Paranormal*. Bristol: Paranthropology. (p. 73).

67 Jokic, Z. (2008). "Yanomami Shamanic Initiation: The Meaning of Death and Postmortem Consciousness in Transformation." *Anthropology of Consciousness*, Vol. 19, No. 1, pp. 33-59.

[68] Eliade, M. (1989). *Shamanism: Archaic Techniques of Ecstasy*. London: Penguin.

[69] Hancock, G. (2005). *Supernatural: Meetings With the Ancient Teachers of Mankind*. London: Arrow Books. (pp. 83-114).

[70] Noll, R. & Shi, K. (2004). 'Chuonnasuan (Meng Jin Fu): The Last Shaman of the Oroqen of Northeast China.' *Journal of Korean Religions*, Vol. 6, pp. 135-162.

[71] Jokic, Z. (2008). "Yanomami Shamanic Initiation: The Meaning of Death and Postmortem Consciousness in Transformation." *Anthropology of Consciousness*, Vol. 19, No. 1, pp. 33-59.

[72] Levi-Strauss, C. (1986). *Structural Anthropology, Volume I*. Harmondsworth: Penguin Books.

[73] Winkelman, M. (1986). 'Shamanic Guidelines for Psychedelic Medicine.' In M. Winkelman & T. Roberts (eds.) *Psychedelic medicine: New evidence for hallucinogenic substances as treatments*. Westport: Praeger. (p. 149)

[74] Brunton, B. (2003). 'The Re-Awakening of Shamanism in the West.' *Shamanism*, Vol. 16, No. 2, pp. 1-5.

[75] Jilek, W.G. (2005). 'Transforming the Shaman: Changing Western Views of Shamanism and Altered States of Consciousness.' *Artemisa*, Vol. 8, No. 1, pp. 8-15.

[76] Hutton, R. (2006). 'Shamanism: Mapping the Boundaries.' *Magic, Ritual and Witchcraft*, Vol. 1, No. 2, pp. 209-213.

[77] McClenon, J. (2012). 'Anthropology, Evolution and Anomalous Experience.' In J. Hunter (ed.) *Paranthropology: Anthropological Approaches to the Paranormal*. Bristol: Paranthropology. (pp. 109-110).

[78] Winkelman, M. (2012). 'Paradigms and Methodologies for Anomalous Research.' In J. Hunter (ed.). *Paranthropology: Anthropological Approaches to the Paranormal*. Bristol: Paranthropology. (pp. 203-206).

[79] Gauld, A. (1982). *Mediumship and Survival: A Century of Investigations*. London: Paladin Books. (p. 29-31).

[80] Bourguignon, E. (1973). *Religion, Altered States of Consciousness and Social Change*. Columbus: Ohio State University Press.

[81] Freed, S.A. & Freed, R.S. (1964). 'Spirit Possession as Illness in a North Indian Village.' *Ethnology*, Vol. 3, No. 2, pp. 152-171.

[82] Schmidt, B. (2016). *Spirits and Trance in Brazil: An Anthropology of Religious Experience*. London: Bloomsbury.

[83] Bird-David, N. (1999). 'Animism Revisited: Personhood, Environment and Relational Epistemology.' *Current Anthropology*, Vol. 40, Supplement, pp. 67-91.

[84] Bubandt, N. (2009). 'Interview with an ancestor: Spirits as informants and the politics of possession in North Maluku.' *Ethnography*, Vol. 10, No. 3, pp. 291-316.

[85] Eliade, M. (1989). *Shamanism: Archaic Techniques of Ecstasy*. London: Penguin. (p.6).

[86] Jokic, Z. (2008). "The Wrath of the Forgotten Ongons: Shamanic Sickness, Spirit Embodiment, and Fragmentary Trancescape in Contemporary Buriat Shamanism." *Sibirica*, Vol. 7, No. 1, pp. 23-50.

[87] Stoller, P. (1992). "Embodying Cultural Memory in Songhay Spirit Possession." *Archives de sciences sociales des religions*, Vol. 79, pp. 53-68.

[88] Rasmussen, S.J. (1994). "The 'Head Dance': Contested Self, and Art as Balancing Act in Tuareg Spirit Possession." *Africa: Journal of the International African Institute*, Vol. 64, No. 1, pp. 74-98.

[89] Leacock, S & Leacock, R. (1975). *Spirits of the Deep: A Study of an Afro-Brazilian Cult*. New York: Anchor Press. (pp. 171-172).

[90] Firth, R. (1967). "Ritual and Drama in Malay Spirit Mediumship." *Comparative Studies in Society and History*, Vol. 9, No. 2, pp. 190-207.

[91] Schechner, R. (1988). *Performance Theory*. London: Routledge.

[92] Spencer, H. (1897). *Principles of Sociology*. New York: D. Appleton and Company. (p. 227).

[93] Crabtree, A. (1988). *Multiple Man: Explorations in Possession and Multiple Personality*. London: Grafton Books.

[94] Oohashi, T., Kawai, N., Honda, M., Nakamura, S., Morimoto, M., Nishina, E., & Maekawa, T. (2002). 'Electroencephalographic Measurement of Possession Trance in the Field.' *Clinical Neurophysiology*, Vol. 112, pp. 435-445.

95 Klass, M. (2003). *Mind Over Mind: The Anthropology and Psychology of Spirit Possession.* Oxford: Rowman & Littlefield. (pp. 118-119).

96 Kilson, M. (1971). "Ambivalence and Power: Mediums in Ga Traditional Religion." *Journal of Religion in Africa,* Vol. 4, pp. 171-177.

97 Lewis, I. M. (1971). *Ecstatic Religion: An Anthropological Study of Spirit Possession and Shamanism.* London: Penguin Books.

98 Cohen, E. (2008). 'What is Spirit Possession? Defining, Comparing and Explaining Two Possession Forms.' *Ethos,* Vol. 73, No. 1, pp. 101-126.

99 Boddy, J. (1988). "Spirits and Selves in Northern Sudan: The Cultural Therapeutics of Possession and Trance." *American Ethnologist,* Vol. 15, No. 1, pp. 4-27.

100 Halloy, A. (2010) "Comments on 'The Mind Possessed: The Cognition of Spirit Possession in an Afro-Brazilian Religious Tradition' by Emma Cohen." *Religion and Society: Advances in Research,* Vol. 1, pp. 164-176.

101 De Jong, A. (1997). *Traditions of the Magi: Zoroastrianism in Greek and Latin Literature.* Leiden: Brill. (pp. 387-403).

102 Bailey, M.D. (2006). 'The Meanings of Magic.' *Magic, Ritual, and Witchcraft,* Vol. 1, No. 1, pp. 1-23.

103 Holt, N.J., Simmons-Moore, C., Luke, D. & French, C.C. (2012). *Anomalistic Psychology.* London: Palgrave Macmillan. (p. 201).

104 Hutton, R. (1999). *The Triumph of the Moon: A History of Modern Pagan Witchcraft.* Oxford: Oxford University Press. (pp. 85-86).

105 Campion, N. (2012). *Astrology and Cosmology in the World's Religions.* New York: New York University Press.

106 Fortes, M. (1982). 'Talensi Divination.' Available Online: http://www.youtube.com/watch?v=9EVj63NYJME [Accessed 29/01/2020].

107 Evans-Pritchard, E.E. (1976). *Witchcraft Oracles and Magic Among the Azande.* Oxford: Clarendon Press.

108 Pearlman, Ellen (2002). *Tibetan Sacred Dance: A Journey Into the Religious and Folk Traditions in Tibet.* Rochester, Vermont: Inner Traditions. (pp. 94-95)

109 Bubandt, N. (2009). "Interview with an Ancestor: Spirits as Informants and the Politics of Possession in North Maluku." *Ethnography,* Vol. 10, No. 3, pp. 291-316.

[110] Winkelman, M. (1986). 'Magico-Religious Practitioner Types and Socioeconomic Conditions.' *Cross-Cultural Research*, No. 20, pp. 17-46.

[111] Stoller, P. & Olkes, C. (1989). *In Sorcery's Shadow*. Chicago: University of Chicago Press. (p. 148).

[112] Kessler, G. (2012). *Fifty Key Thinkers on Religion*. London: Routledge. (p. 41).

[113] Frazer, J.G. (1993). *The Golden Bough: A Study in Magic and Religion*. Ware: Wordsworth Editions.

[114] Mauss, M. (2001) *A General Theory of Magic*. London: Routledge. (pp. 16, 160-161, 174).

[115] Ralley, R. (2010). *Magic: A Beginners Guide*. Oxford: Oneworld. (pp. 142-143).

[116] Berger, P.L. (1971). *A Rumour of Angels: Modern Society and the Rediscovery of the Supernatural*. London: Penguin Books.

[117] Partridge, C. (2005). *The Re-Enchantment of the West Vol. 1: Alternative Spiritualities, Sacralization, Popular Culture and Occulture*. London: Bloomsbury.

[118] Hutton, R. (1999). *The Triumph of the Moon: A History of Modern Pagan Witchcraft*. Oxford: Oxford University Press. (p. 241).

[119] Bowie, F. (2001). *The Anthropology of Religion*. Oxford: Blackwell.

[110] Hole, C. (1977). *Witchcraft in England*. London: B.T. Batsford.

[121] Wilby, E. (2010). *The Visions of Isobel Gowdie: Magic, Witchcraft and Dark Shamanism in Seventeenth-Century Scotland*. Brighton: Sussex Academic Press.

[122] Evans-Pritchard, E.E. (1976). *Witchcraft Oracles and Magic Among the Azande*. Oxford: Clarendon Press.

[123] Favret-Saada, J. (2010). *Deadly Words: Witchcraft in the Bocage*. Cambridge: Cambridge University Press.

[124] Bowie, F. (2001). *The Anthropology of Religion*. Oxford: Blackwell. (pp. 235-240).

[125] Hutton, R. (1999). *The Triumph of the Moon: A History of Modern Pagan Witchcraft*. Oxford: Oxford University Press. (p. 205-206).

126 Stewart, P. J. & Strathern, A. (2004). *Witchcraft, Sorcery, Rumours and Gossip.* Cambridge: Cambridge University Press.

127 Stocking Jr, G.W. (1971). "Animism in Theory and Practice: E.B. Tylor's Unpublished Notes on Spiritualism." *Man.* Vol. 6, No. 1, pp. 88-104.

128 Evans-Pritchard, E.E. (1976). *Witchcraft Oracles and Magic Among the Azande.* Oxford: Clarendon Press.

129 Grindal, B.T. (1983). 'Into the Heart of Sisala Experience: Witnessing Death Divination.' *Journal of Anthropological Research*, Vol. 39, No. 1, pp. 60-80.

130 Turner, E. (1993). 'The Reality of Spirits: A Tabooed or Permitted Field of Study?' *Anthropology of Consciousness*, Vol. 4, No. 1, pp. 9-12.

131 Mousalimas, S.A. (1990). 'The concept of participation in Lévy-Bruhl's 'Primitive Mentality." *Journal of the Anthropological Society of Oxford*, Vol. 21, No. 1, pp. 33-46.

132 Bowie, F. (2012). "Devising Methods for the Ethnographic Study of the Afterlife: Cognition, Empathy and Engagement." In J. Hunter (ed.) *Paranthropology: Anthropological Approaches to the Paranormal.* Bristol: Paranthropology. (pp. 99-106).

133 Eagleman, D. (nd.) "Possibilianism." Available Online: http://www.possibilian.com [Accessed 29/01/2020].

134 Hunter, J. (2015). '"Between Realness and Unrealness": Anthropology, Parapsychology and the Ontology of Non-Ordinary Realities.' *Diskus: Journal of the British Association for the Study of Religion*, Vol. 17, No. 2, pp. 4-20.

135 Melechi, A. (2003). *Fugitive Minds: On Madness, Sleep and Other Twilight Afflictions.* London: William Heinemann. (pp. 129-136).

136 Crabtree, A. (1988). *Multiple Man: Explorations in Possession and Multiple Personality.* London: Grafton Books. (pp. 22-24).

137 Melechi, A. (2008). *Servants of the Supernatural: The Night Side of the Victorian Mind.* London: William Heinemann. (pp. 110-114).

138 Taves, A. (1999). *Fits, Trances and Visions: Experiencing Religion and Explaining Experience from Wesley to James.* Princeton: Princeton University Press. (p. 248).

[139] Moreman, C.M. (2010). *Beyond the Threshold: Afterlife Beliefs and Experiences in World Religions.* Lanham: Rowman & Littlefield. (pp. 161-162).

[140] Lamont, P. (2005). *The First Psychic: The Peculiar Mystery of a Notorious Victorian Wizard.* London: Abacus.

[141] Alvarado, C.S. (2006). "Human Radiations: Concepts of Force in Mesmerism, Spiritualism and Psychical Research." *Journal of the Society for Psychical Research,* Vol. 70, No. 884, pp. 138-162.

[142] Kripal, J. (2011). *Authors of the Impossible: The Paranormal and the Sacred.* Chicago: University of Chicago Press. (p. 80).

[143] Broughton, R. (1991). *Parapsychology: The Controversial Science.* London: Rider Books. (p. 47).

[144] Holt, N.J., Simmonds-Moore, C., Luke, D. & French, C. (2012). *Anomalistic Psychology.* London: Palgrave Macmillan. (pp. 112-113).

[145] Radin, D. (2006). *Entangled Minds: Extrasensory Experiences in a Quantum Reality.* New York: Paraview Pocket Books. (pp. 120-121).

[146] Radin, D. (2006). *Entangled Minds: Extrasensory Experiences in a Quantum Reality.* New York: Paraview Pocket Books. (pp. 120-121).

[147] Holt *et al., Anomalistic Psychology,* pp. 106-111.

[148] Holt *et al., Anomalistic Psychology,* pp. 26-27.

[149] Coxhead, N. (1979). *Mindpower.* Harmondsworth: Penguin Books. (pp. 30-31).

[150] Walsh, K. & Moddel, G. (2007). "Effect of Belief on Psi Performance in a Card Guessing Task." *Journal of Scientific Exploration,* Vol. 21, No. 3, pp. 501-510.

[151] Lawrence, T. (1993). "Gathering in the sheep and goats: A meta-analysis of forced-choice sheep-goat ESP studies, 1947-1993." In *Proceedings of Presented Papers: The Parapsychological Association 36th Annual Convention* (pp. 75-86).

[152] Bem, D. (2011). 'Feeling the Future: Experimental Evidence for Anomalous Retroactive Influences on Cognition and Affect.' *Journal of Personality and Social Psychology,* Vol. 100, pp. 407-425.

[153] Batcheldor, K.J. (1984). "Contributions to the theory of PK induction from sitter-group work." *Journal of the American Society for Psychical Research,* Vol 78, No. 2, pp. 105-122.

[154] Storm, L. & Thalbourne, M.A. (2000). 'A Paradigm Shift Away from the ESP-PK Dichotomy: The Theory of Psychopraxia.' *Journal of Parapsychology*, Vol. 64, pp. 279-300.

[155] Klimo, J. (1987). *Channeling: Investigations on Receiving Information from Paranormal Sources.* Los Angeles: Jeremy P. Tarcher Inc. (p. 200).

[156] Braude, S. (1997). *The Limits of Influence: Psychokinesis and the Philosophy of Science.* New York: University Press of America.

[157] Rogo, D.S. (1988). *The Infinite Boundary: Spirit Possession, Madness, and Multiple Personality.* Wellingborough: The Aquarian Press. (pp. 32-33).

[158] Beischel, J. (2008). 'Contemporary Methods Used in Laboratory Mediumship Research.' *Journal of Parapsychology*, Vol. 71, pp. 37-68.

[159] Muldoon, S. & Carrington, H. (1973 [1951]). *The Phenomena of Astral Projection.* London: Rider & Company.

[160] Monroe, R.A. (1972). *Journeys Out of the Body.* London: Souvenir Press. (pp. 60-75).

[161] Moody, R. (1975). *Life After Life.* Covington: Mockingbird Books.

[162] Sartori, P., Badham, P. & Fenwick, P. (2006). 'A Prospectively Studied Near-Death Experience with Corroborated Out-of-Body Perceptions and Unexplained Healing.' *Journal of Near-Death Studies*, Vol. 25, No. 2, pp. 69-84.

[163] Blackmore, S. (1993). *Dying to Live: Science and the Near-Death Experience.* London: Grafton.

[164] Schlitz, M., Wiseman, R., Watt, C. & Radin, D. (2006). 'Of Two Minds: Sceptic-Proponent Collaboration Within Parapsychology.' *British Journal of Parapsychology*, Vol. 97, pp. 313-322.

[165] Luke, D. (2010). 'Anthropology and Parapsychology: Still Hostile Sisters in Science?' *Time and Mind*, Vol. 3, No. 3, pp. 245-265.

[166] Lang, A. (2010). *Cock Lane and Common Sense.* Bibliobazaar, LLC. (p. 19).

[167] de Martino, E. (1972). *Magic: Primitive and Modern.* London: Tom Stacey.

[168] Long, J. K. (ed.) (1977). *Extrasensory Ecology: Parapsychology and Anthropology.* Metuchen: Scarecrow Press.

[169] Angoff, A. & Barth, D. (eds.) (1974). *Parapsychology and Anthropology: Proceedings of an International Conference.* New York: Parapsychology Foundation.

[170] Society for the Anthropology of Consciousness (nd.) Available Online: https://anthrosource.onlinelibrary.wiley.com/hub/journal/15563537/about/society-information/ [Accessed 29/01/2020].

[171] Schroll, M.A. & Schwartz, S. (2005). 'Whither Psi and Anthropology? An Incomplete History of SACs Origins, its Relationship with Transpersonal Psychology and the Untold Stories of Castaneda's Controversy.' *Anthropology of Consciousness*, Vol. 16, No. 1, pp. 6-24.

[172] Laughlin, C. (2012). 'Transpersonal Anthropology: What Is It, and What are the Problems we Face Doing It?' In J. Hunter (ed.) *Paranthropology: Anthropological Approaches to the Paranormal.* Bristol: Paranthropology. (pp. 70-74).

[173] Laughlin, C. (1997). 'The Cycle of Meaning: Some Methodological Implications of Biogenetic Structural Theory.' In S. Glazier (ed.) *Anthropology of Religion: Handbook of Theory and Method.* Westport: Greenwood Press.

[174] Giesler, P., (1984). 'Parapsychological Anthropology: I. Multi-method Approaches to the Study of Psi in the Field Setting.' *Journal of the American Society for Psychical Research*, Vol. 78, pp. 287-328.

[175] Young, D.E. & Goulet, J-G. (1994). *Being Changed by Cross-Cultural Encounters: The Anthropology of Extraordinary Experience.* Ontario: Broadview Press. (p. 12).

[176] Hunter, J. (ed.) (2012). *Paranthropology: Anthropological Approaches to the Paranormal.* Bristol: Paranthropology.

[177] Graham, F (2011). 'Commentary on "Reflecting on Paranthropology."' *Paranthropology: Journal of Anthropological Approaches to the Paranormal*, Vol. 2, No. 3, pp 20-21.

[178] Luke, D. (2012). 'Experiential Reclamation and First-Person Parapsychology.' In J. Hunter (ed.) *Paranthropology: Anthropological Approaches to the Paranormal.* Bristol: Paranthropology.

[179] Luke, D. (2011). 'Anomalous Phenomena, Psi and Altered Consciousness.' In E. Cardeña, and M. Winkelman (eds.) *Altering Consciousness: A Multidisciplinary Perspective, Volume 2 – Biological and Psychological Perspectives.* Westport: Praeger. (pp.355-374).

[180] Myers, F.W.H. (1992). *Human Personality and its Survival of Bodily Death*. Norwich: Pelegrin Trust.

[181] Kelly, E.F. & Locke, R.G. (2009). *Altered States of Consciousness and Psi: An Historical Survey and Research Prospectus*. New York: Parapsychology Foundation.

[182] Bourguignon, E. (1973). "A Framework for the Comparative Study of Altered States of Consciousness." In E. Bourguignon (ed.) *Religion, Altered States of Consciousness and Social Change*. Columbus: Ohio State University Press. (pp. 3-38).

[183] Grindal, B.T. (1983). 'Into the Heart of Sisala Experience: Witnessing Death Divination.' *Journal of Anthropological Research*, Vol. 39, No. 1, pp. 60-80.

[184] Turner, E. (1998). *Experiencing Ritual: A New Interpretation of African Healing*. Philadelphia: University of Pennsylvania Press.

[185] Levi-Strauss, C. (1986). *Structural Anthropology 1*. Harmondsworth: Penguin Books. (p. 168).

[186] Kiev, A. (1972). *Transcultural Psychiatry*. Harmondsworth: Penguin Books. (pp. 78-108).

[187] Hustvedt, S. (2011). *Medical Muses: Hysteria in Nineteenth Century Paris*. London: Bloomsbury.

[188] van de Port, M. (2011). *Ecstatic Encounters: Bahian Candomble and the Quest for the Really Real*. Amsterdam: Amsterdam University Press.

[189] Haldane, J.B.S., (1927). *Possible worlds and other papers*. London: Chatto & Windus. (p. 286).

[190] Long, J. K. (1977). 'Parapsychology in Anthropology (or, Don Juan's Separate Reality Revisited)'. In J. K. Long (ed.). *Extrasensory Ecology: Parapsychology and Anthropology*. Metuchen: Scarecrow Press. (pp. 1–11).

[191] James, W. (1996). *Essays in radical empiricism*. Lincoln: University of Nebraska Press. (p. 42).

INDEX

~